Do
Not
Interrupt
Your
Activities

an exhibition curated by
graduating students
on the Curating Contemporary Art MA

NOT INTERRU

Royal College of Art 2005

The exhibition would not have been possible without the generous support of the following:

Sponsorship-in-kind provided by:

Chinese Arts Centre
华人艺术中心

LAURA BARTLETT GALLERY

GOETHE-INSTITUT
LONDON

ⒾASPIS

Premier Paper

specialblue

4

Contents

INTERRUPT Y

Preface

Solitary acts, social acts, communicative acts, critical acts, constructive acts.
A disparate range of activities, of temperaments and voices, of cultural situations
and exigencies, is represented in the works brought together for this exhibition.
They do not conform to a single thematic or share a consistent mood, but connect
with each other singly or in small clusters, offering a range of reflections on
personal, political and social dilemmas. Some of these works address their contexts
symbolically or metaphorically, some more directly. Some are absorbed and
introspective, others expansive and sociable. Many speak of the need to register
acts of resistance or reflection, and of the responsibilities associated with any
action undertaken in the world.

This is the first exhibition made by curators on the MA Curating Contemporary Art
in which performance and live art have played a significant role, presented as an
integral part of the exhibition and of the accompanying catalogue. Many of the live
events are self-evidently performative and participatory, but there are also works
in the galleries that adopt performance procedures, or that direct attention to the
conventions of performance within contemporary society.

The starting point for the discussion about the exhibition was a 'retreat' to the
Lake District, where the curatorial group stayed in a house owned by Grizedale
Arts. Alistair Hudson and Adam Sutherland acted as hosts for this trip, as well as
providing good company and conversation. As in previous years, the exhibition
incorporates the contributions of many such individuals, who have provided
help and advice with different aspects of the exhibition. Their names are given
on page 115.

The Curating Contemporary Art Department has followed the initiative pioneered last year and has again engaged a visiting curator to mentor the curatorial group through the conception and realisation of their exhibition. The Berlin-based curator and critic Astrid Mania has joined the department for five months, bringing with her new perspectives and expertise. We are deeply grateful for the intelligence and commitment she has brought to her work with us, and for the subtlety of her understanding of this demanding role.

The catalogue for this exhibition has been designed by Peter B. Willberg, who is also responsible for the overall graphic identity of the exhibition. We are grateful to Peter for his long-term engagement with the work of the department, and for the outstanding contribution he has made as both designer and teacher. Similarly we should like to record our thanks to our printers, Specialblue, for their generous support for the annual exhibition catalogue.

We should also like to express our thanks to Arts Council England, which has co-funded the course since its inauguration in 1992, and to the John Lyon's Charity, another long-standing benefactor. Cultural agencies that have kindly provided grants and help-in-kind for this exhibition are acknowledged on page 4.

And finally we should like to thank the artists for their imaginative involvement with this exhibition project, their companionship and support.

Teresa Gleadowe

ES DO NOT IN

Introduction

Without making grand statements, the works in *Do Not Interrupt Your Activities* seep into our consciousness. They give new weight and meaning to small-scale activities. They try to think about ways in which the world might be made more tolerable, or at least to consider whether this is possible. Theirs is a strategy in which resistance and futility are finely balanced; they assert a fragile presence in the face of current realities. Sometimes this embraces an almost therapeutic need to make work. Sachiko Abe indulges in an obsessive activity of paper cutting, which is both her art work and a means of coping with the exterior world.

Many of the works in this exhibition ask us to examine things we take for granted – freedom of speech and of movement and expression. Others look at the social and political conditions that shape our behaviour and the way we act in society: Johanna Billing's video is a striking metaphor for the condition of her generation, a youth suspended in painful indecision, whereas David Hatcher's plaques of governmental 'expectations' as to the citizen's responsibilities look at how our behaviour is shaped. Other artists develop strategies to deal with contemporary pressures: Song Dong invites us to write with water what we would otherwise not dare to express, while Emily Jacir's caustic project *Sexy Semite* uses black humour to highlight harsh political restrictions.

Many of the artists in this exhibition use parody and absurdity as critical weapons. Roman Ondák's *Announcement* evokes the one-minute silence or propaganda announcement: 'As a sign of solidarity with recent world events, for the next minute do not interrupt the activity you are doing at this moment'. Ondák's request holds the audience in a double-bind: any action automatically obeys his command, and he also takes credit for our continuing activity. His piece generates confusion,

ERRUPT YOUR

asking for neither respectful pause nor rebellion against the status quo, but simply instructing us to continue as we are.

The works in *Do Not Interrupt Your Activities* are organised around an idea of performance: actions, hesitations, refusals, gestures. Some works are live performances, others record or restage earlier actions, others merely contemplate the possibility and efficacy of any kind of activity. Some are documentary, like Leopold Kessler's records of his urban interventions, while others are constructions, like Deimantas Narkevičius's fictitious reworking of Lithuania's post-Soviet history.

The performances and live events in *Do Not Interrupt Your Activities* have a markedly different relationship with their audience from the confrontational, at times aggressive, performances and happenings of the 60s and 70s. The live artists of today seek to develop a more ambiguous relationship with their viewers. Shock and abjection are less commonly used. The body is no longer an unmediated vehicle of expression, a battlefield of societal and political change. Instead, Robin Deacon and Richard Dedomenici use their bodies to exploit the clichés of performance art. Yara El-Sherbini, Reader and Talkaoke adopt and parody the political instruments of democracy – the roundtable discussion, the workshop, the symposium or debate – without any expectation that these artistic endeavours will result in a call to arms.

But the works in *Do Not Interrupt Your Activities* also set themselves apart from recent tendencies in contemporary art: work that reaches out to specific communities that do not conventionally constitute the gallery-going public; work that emphasises conviviality; work that uses game-playing as a metaphor for global political systems. While Nicolas Bourriaud contends that the viewer takes what

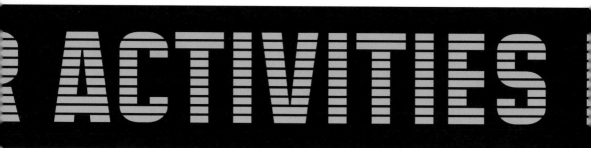

he has learnt in the gallery space out into the 'real' world, that the gallery offers
a space in which genuine relations can be shaped, the art work included in this
exhibition appears to engage with society in rather different ways.

This is not to say that the work in *Do Not Interrupt Your Activities* altogether rejects
the possibility that art might facilitate social change; rather, it incorporates within
it the acknowledgment that art can operate on more complex levels. Art can give
you, the individual viewer, an alternative way of looking at the world around you. So
if it is political, it is no more than potentially so; political because a personal action,
made by the artist and expressed in the work, has a resonance with the viewer.

In a recent article on the relationship between art and politics, the critic Jan
Verwoert argues that in the current political climate there is an overwhelming
pressure to be for or against a given ideological standpoint. Yet, for Verwoert, an
alternative position does exist – it is that of the sceptic, who tries 'to step back
from choice, play for time, and thus sabotage the mechanism by which power and
its systems of logic are enforced'. In harnessing this position, art and intellectual
discourse have the capacity to 'disarm, touch and disconcert.'[1] This approach
seems to highlight the power implicit in choosing not to act, a hesitation that might
open up a space for critical reflection. In this context, Ondák's *Announcement*
makes us self-conscious and invites us to reassess our potential for positive
(in)action.

Rose Lejeune and Ali MacGilp

1 Jan Verwoert, *Frieze*, November/December 2004,
issue 87, p 83

RUPT YOUR AC

Live Art – A Conversation
Sarah McCrory and Rebecca May Marston

RMM: Shall we begin by discussing how the idea of our exhibition came about in the first place? Why do we have a live events programme? Why has performance been so important to our discussions from the beginning?

SM: In the very beginning we talked about making an exhibition about performance, which would have included references to its history.

RMM: There have been a number of exhibitions that revisited performance during the 1960s and 1970s, for instance *Video Acts* at the ICA, and *A Short History of Performance* at the Whitechapel and Jens Hoffman's series of representations and reinterpretations, *A Little Bit of History Repeated*. But we really wanted to focus on contemporary performance and make space for some critical discussion.

SM: We were interested to know what the concerns of contemporary performance artists are. Why is performance or live art again so prevalent, although the concerns of the past have changed? In the early days, artists attempted to escape the commercial system of the art gallery, they thought that through performance they would have a direct impact on society.

RMM: The unmediated expression of their ideas still makes performance attractive for artists today. It also has the ability to make a series of demands upon the audience.

SM: Performance *is* challenging. It demands time and it can be very uncomfortable to watch.

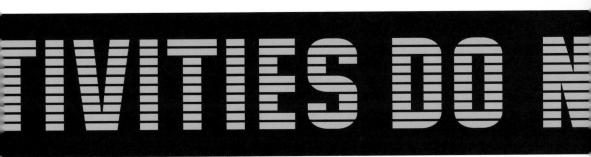

RMM: Video also demands your time, but it can't make you sit down and watch, whereas walking away from a performance really is difficult. You, as the audience, are part of that work, you complete it.

SM: I think the discomfort is to do with self-consciousness. I find it really interesting that performance still has that ability to confront. Performance, or live art as it is referred to by most artists today, does still have that impact. I do still squirm. Sometimes, I have to stand there and ask 'why is this interesting?'.

RMM: It's a leap of faith, in a way, as everybody involved has to surrender some control. I think performance work is fundamentally about power and responsibility and the self-consciousness of the performer and the audience.

SM: Definitely, I think that power oscillates in the relationship between the performer and the audience. A lecture performance has a very definite set of values concerning its power structure, and artists such as Richard Dedomenici, exploit that. When he makes his artistic failures the subject of his performance, he undermines himself, while at the same time the didactic lecture format gives him a certain degree of authority. Mikey Weinkove from Talkaoke prides himself on his ability to 'man the table' as a chairperson and host. Once he lets his guard down as adjudicator, he gives into a loss of control. In the visual arts the artist has total control, but in performance there's a 'liveness' that embraces accidents and mistakes and all of those nuances that change the work. That's the beauty of performance, you can see a single piece three times and it will be different every time.

RMM: The members of the performance group *Reader* openly profess to both 'charm and terrorise' their audience, and they prove extremely alluring

OT INTERRUP

manipulators. My last encounter with their work was a situation of intense discomfort. They had created a fake tour of Canada projected onto the streets of Glasgow and so I found myself alone, in a dark alley, sitting on a camping chair whilst listening to one of the group's soothing tones describing the rivers of vomit running down the streets on Friday nights.

SM: I think it's really important to ask how relationships are forged when programming live acts as we're so used to examining the relationships between works in exhibitions. You've been to live art festivals, so maybe you can talk a bit about how they are curated with regard to subject rather than practicalities.

RMM: It seems to me that most live art festivals are not curated in the sense of tying works together and establishing connections between them. While more general themes such as the body or events that involve a one-to-one relationship between performer and audience member are quite common, it is much more unusual to programme with emphasis on subtler interconnections between works.

SM: We are committed to integrating live works into the concept of our exhibition. I'm sure there have been other shows that have incorporated performance into them, but we're trying to give the live art equal weight, conceptually and physically, weaving the events into the fabric of the exhibition. It is no accident that we have a live presence throughout the duration of the exhibition with Sachiko Abe's *Cut Papers*.

RMM: There have been recent examples of live art shown in galleries and museums, like *Live at Tate*, which was curated in association with the Live Art Development Agency. It was very successful and brought live works to a new public. However it was presented as a live art festival within Tate, rather than a

YOUR ACTIVI

foray into the curating of live work and other visual art forms in an integrated way. We're hoping that people will consider the work sited in the gallery and the live works as inextricably linked. I think the immediacy of the live events will add urgency to these more mediated acts.

SM: But all the artists in *Do Not Interrupt Your Activities* seem to acknowledge a degree of political powerlessness, which mirrors our experience as individuals – a good example of which was the futile gesture of marching against the war in Iraq – and yet they also all share a feeling of necessity and a determination to continue making their work.

RMM: Exactly. This is where our exhibition integrates the characteristics of performance with the ideas our artists are addressing.

SM: And the commitment to process rather than product, in all performance work, has explicit connections with the acts we've looked at. These ideas are a cross-section of the range of acts we've examined and have found to be potent, often in process rather than outcome. The result has always been less important for us than the action.

RMM: This emphasis on process embraces the idea of futility. As we've said before, in the 1960s and 1970s artists believed they might change the world. Now artists know they can't but they continue to act anyway. That's the crux of our show.

TIES DO NOT

Sachiko Abe

Johanna Billing

Pavel Braìla

Lali Chetwynd

Kim Coleman &

Jenny Hogarth

Robin Deacon

Richard Dedomenici

Harrell Fletcher

David Hatcher

Emily Jacir

Jesper Just

Leopold Kessler

Deimantas Narkevičius

Roman Ondák

Michael Rakowitz

Reader

Giorgio Sadotti

Yara El-Sherbini

Christian Sievers

Song Dong

Kate Stannard

Talkaoke

Mark Wayman

Sachiko Abe (b 1975)

Sachiko Abe's biography is indivisible from her current artistic practice. Growing up in Japan, she spent a period of her teens forcibly confined in a mental institution, and the work that she has performed in recent exhibitions and now again at the Royal College of Art is a response to this experience. It is the artist's technique for keeping her mind balanced from day to day as much as it is an art practice.

Cocooned in a softly-lit gauze chamber, a sactuary cut off from the world outside, Abe practices her obsessive task. She sits and cuts paper in strips every day for periods of up to ten hours. The paper, which varies between thicknesses of 0.3 and 0.5mm and can go to lengths of 5.30m, builds up around her, creating a highly delicate but dense white mass that seems to act as a protective blanket. The act of cutting paper is a product of the artist's time in hospital and has been her almost daily task for nearly ten years, providing her with a process of dealing with the thoughts in her head. The sound of the scissors, transported in and out of the space, provides her with some sort of comfort and allows her to dispel thoughts of harming herself. The length and thickness of the strip depends on the level of importance of the thought; the goal is not to cut them thin or long but simply to perform the act. Abe's creative process is fuelled by her unique introspective

Cut Papers, 2005
Continuous performance with various materials
Courtesy of Laura Bartlett Gallery

reality. She displaces her emotion into a physical form; the cutting of paper. The act of sublimation, a process that has been described by Louise Bourgeois as 'a gift', is the impulse behind her work.

The creation of something as delicate as strips of paper using an object that could potentially be very harmful sets up a tension throughout the work. Inside the institution Abe's scissors were at first continually taken away from her, causing her to beg her visitors to bring her more. Paradoxically, it is the harmful scissors that provide her with comfort. Further, her act is brutal – she destroys something, and yet it takes away her pain. Her act and tools are aggressive and yet they provide her with a form of protection.

Abe sees her work as being different from other artistic practices. Despite creating a very beautiful installation, that creation is more about process than product and, above all, it was not originally intended as an art work. Abe has worked as a visual artist for some years and has made various performances, but only recently began showing this particular activity. It is interesting to question why she felt compelled to shift it into the context of the art gallery.

Formalising self-expression is fundamental to the performing arts in Japanese culture. The Kabuki theatre, which originated in the seventeenth century, emerged as a means for artists to express their emotions, against the background of a society they felt did not permit this. Butoh dance, which emerged as a response to the Second World War, is a modern dance practice that offered a new means of expression to its practitioners, unencumbered by language, custom or restriction.

The idea of the action being the most significant part of the art work was inherent in the practice of the Japanese Gutai group or 'Concrete Art Association'. Formed in 1954, their practice centered on the act of making the work, process rather product. Their performances were limited to the presentation of art that was time-based.

Perhaps the most important forerunner for Abe's work is fellow Japanese artist Yayoi Kusama. Like Abe, Kusama describes her work as a form of self-therapy to overcome childhood trauma. Kusama's work, primarily painting and installations with endless spots and polka dots, is born out of the hallucinations she has experienced all her life. She sees her work at an 'attempt at artistic creation based on the inevitability that emerged within me.'[1]

Abe's fashioning of a personal practice into a work of art creates a space that is so intimate that a tacit contract is established between artist and viewer. On entering Abe's chamber the viewer might feel like an intruder and yet the calm of the situation means they soon relax. They are then free to enjoy the ethereal vision before them. The visitor might be reminded of tales of medieval princesses shrouded in their bowers or of Sleeping Beauty dreaming in a castle surrounded by thorns.

Giselle Richardson

[1] Yayoi Kusama 'The Struggle and Wanderings of My Soul (extracts) 1975', from Laura Hoptman et al, *Yayoi Kusama*, Phaidon Press London, 2000 pp 118–122

Johanna Billing (b 1973)

Watching and waiting are central to Johanna Billing's *Where she is at* (2001), a seven minute loop that charts a girl's progress on a high diving platform. The film is composed of short cuts that focus on different elements of the scene, piecing together the whole picture through a series of isolated fragments incompatible with any one perspective. We see her make her way down a shady gravel track to the beach; climb to the top of the diving tower; then balk, unable to make the leap. Shots of her alternately wincing and inching her way to the edge, testing herself against the railings and sitting defeated, legs hanging over the ledge, are inter-spersed with those of people on the beach watching her torment or just doing their own thing. Wind on the water and the sounds of birds can be heard, other people make their way to the beach, and second by second her discomfort builds up until, finally, she jumps. Resurfacing below, she emerges from the water, re-walks the jetty, re-climbs the diving tower, reaches the top and balks, unable to take the leap...

Time, felt so heavily for all of the minutes of her indecision, trips up on itself, trapping the girl in the spell of its loop. This prolonged anticipation and never-ending waiting is typical of Billing's work, which deals with issues of indecision,

Where She Is At, 2001
Video (DV PAL)
Courtesy of the artist

postponement and inertia and which finds its perfect formal representation in the device of the loop. For all the girl's anguished and debilitating deliberation, she achieves more than many of the protagonists in Billing's films who often repeat past actions with conspicuous lack of results. *Project for a Revolution* (2000) is a contemporary take on a scene from Antonioni's 1970s film *Zabriskie Point*. In both, a meeting is underway, but whereas the students in Antonioni's film are disconcertingly rowdy and chaotic, Billing's three minute loop is silent and nothing gets done. Pamphlets are printed blank and people hang around bored, waiting for something to happen. It deals, as Billing suggests, 'with being stuck in something,'[1] and with her own generation's uncertainty as to the wisdom and efficacy of the protest and demonstration practised by their parents in the 60s and early 70s. Born in Sweden in the mid 70s, Billing is part of an age group often criticised for being self-seeking and politically lazy, and her works often communicate the difficulties now faced in knowing how to act. Repetitions and references in the works highlight just how different things now are and these reiterations intimate how much we are doomed to repeat what has already been done.

Missing Out (2001) is another loop. To make it, Billing got a group of twenty-somethings to re-enact a relaxation exercise that she has memories of being made to do at primary school. Again, the differences from the original are pronounced,

Where She Is At, 2001
Video (DV PAL)
Courtesy of the artist

1 Johanna Billing, interview with Anders Jansson,
E-CART, www.e-cart

for the earlier generation's belief in conformity and collective action has apparently been displaced by a contemporary individualism. Required to lie flat on the floor and merely breathe is too much for one of the assembled company. He gets up and walks to the window, unable to stay still with the others. With its young protagonists and slick editing, the film resembles a fashion or advertisement spread. Seen from above these participants spread star-shaped and bright against the white floor resemble patterns as much as people. The spliced together sequence of different camera shots and the overall pattern of the loop sets a monotonous rhythm from which the restless individual tries unsuccessfully to escape. Billing's work stems from the same feeling of being trapped that she inflicts upon her film's protagonists: 'All things I've done come out of the same thing: I feel that we may be living our lives in a way we maybe were not looking for in the first place. The

Missing Out, 2001
Video (DV PAL)
Courtesy of the artist

standards that are put up by society are saying to us that we should always be striving for something, and that we should fulfil ourselves. It's there and then that you discover you are trapped in a pattern that you don't know how to get out of.'[2]

But there are obvious compensations for being one of a group and part of a pattern – shared feelings, love, beauty, for instance. Since 2002 Billing has been addressing the issue of individuals coming together through a song project, *You don't love me yet*. Characteristically, the work revisits a prior event – in this case Roky Erickson's original 1984 song – but has particular resonance used in its new context: Billing was inspired by the knowledge that Sweden currently has more people living alone than in any other country, suggesting a population reluctant to sacrifice independence for family life. The project began as a day-long concert held in Stockholm, in which a hundred local musicians performed, at Billing's invitation, their own versions of the song. Since then it has toured throughout Sweden, always with different bands performing. Despite the sad lyrics, the song is rousingly upbeat. The harmonious conjoining of many individual performers in the chorus wonderfully belies the very words they sing. The key word is *yet*, repeated over and over in the song and still more through the tour. Like the loop in Billing's films, *You don't love me yet* denies resolution, but it also refuses to give up; an incantation that brings people together every time it is sung.

Gair Boase

2 Johanna Billing, interview with Anders Jansson,
E-CART, www.e-cart

Pavel Braìla (b 1971)

The principal leitmotif in Pavel Braìla's work is the traversal of space – physical, emotional, historical. Through his often laborious movement across boundaries he elucidates the gaps, interstices and disconnections of personal and historical narratives providing a diagnosis of a particular moment.

In his earlier works Braìla himself is implicated as a performer in this process of traversal: his body and its stuttering vocabulary of jolts and gestures becomes a conduit for the articulation of history and its cultural and economic legacy. In *Pioneer* (1997), the artist rolls down a hill into a forest with a giant industrial spool of white paper. In *Work* (2000), a barefoot Braìla smothers a marshy section of agricultural land with white paper, drilling holes to plant seeds and thereafter digging over his 'paper field'.

This exhibition features *Recalling Events* (2000). Filmed from above, Braìla enters from camera-left, walking onto a chalkboard. Through an almost ritualized process of mark-making and erasure, Braìla scribbles monumental events, such as his graduation from the Jan van Eyck Academie in Maastricht, onto the board, filtering his own and Moldova's coterminous post-Soviet transition. His body becomes a brush, with each handwritten jerk being wiped away in sync with a frantic rhythm. Sharp scrawl upon scrawl; each undone. As he persists with his almost amnesiac narrative, his clothes become increasingly soiled by the chalk. History catches up with him and his frenetic movements are exhausted. He sheds item upon item of his clothing, leaving folds of cloth and memory trailed across the centre of the board.

Braìla's performance makes memory palpable. His portrayal of history – personally filtered, frantically embodied, and articulated in a state of metamorphosis – is visually hypnotic. Large sections of the black-painted surface, feverishly covered, assert a sense of the exhausting onward march of history and the implication of one man's personal journey within it.

Braìla's physical traversal of space shifts in later pieces from his own body to more abstracted situations, which act as visual metaphors. His move away from the use of his own body is noteworthy mainly because his subject matter does not seem to change. His earlier works actively demonstrate his personal history and, as a Moldovan, the burden of his national heritage. The later works, while dealing with very different subject matter, remain intensely autobiographical.

Road (2001) and *Shoes for Europe* (2002) mark a turning point in Braìla's practice. In the former he accompanies a truck-driver on an overnight journey from West to East – from Maastricht to Chisinau – symbolically bridging class, geographical and political divides. In *Shoes For Europe* Braìla harnesses the idea of the daily commute, to articulate the corporeal reality of the historical differentiation between East and West. Braìla features the small frontier train station of Ungheni, at the Moldovan-Romanian border, where a train's wheels need to be changed from the Russian gauge used in Moldova to the standard gauge used in Romania and Western Europe. Braìla's footage, illegally shot, documents the laborious three-hour changeover, thereby portraying, through very physical and ultimately mundane means, the scars of previous political and ideological battles.

Recalling Events, 2000
DV transfered onto
DVD, 4min.
Courtesy of Galerie
Yvon Lambert, Paris

Braìla's most recent production, *Barons' Hill* (2005), documents the extravagant architectural disneylands that are owned by the Roma people in the Moldovan city of Soroca. The film comprises a series of long, almost languid, tracking shots, visually investigating the grandiose interiors and overblown carapaces of these Roma-owned properties.

Ironically these homes are infrequently inhabited and mainly reserved for holidays and special occasions. Some have been boarded over, seemingly abandoned mid-construction. Many others pay tacky homage to a plethora of architectural and artistic influences, some of which reference the marathon Roma treks from India some fourteen centuries ago: ornamental ceilings reminiscent of the European baroque mix with multi-level overhanging roofs with elaborately wrought decoration resembling Nepalese Hindu temples.

Such ostentatious displays of wealth could indicate a fundamental misunder-standing of the demonstrations of capitalist success. By buying into a system of possession that has little cultural relevance to their own lifestyles, the Roma assert, by way of dramatic irony, the dislocation and fragmentation of their historical identity. Again, Braìla succeeds in finding visual means to narrate a great journey, and its bizarre remains.

James Lindon

Lali Chetwynd (b 1973)

Lali Chetwynd's performances are an absurd spectacle. Before they have even
begun there is chaos. Costumes are frantically glue-gunned to actors, whiskers
hastily re-attached and scenes hurriedly dictated... and it is only two minutes until
'curtain up'. Except that there are no curtains. And there is no stage. There is no
script, and, really, these are not actors.

Involving a cast of amateurs, a host of hand-made costumes and props, and a series
of venues ranging from white cube gallery spaces to squats, Lali Chetwynd's
performances are simultaneously funny, awkward and deadly serious. The subjects
of her performances derive from an educational background in anthropology, a
family background in theatre, and a curiosity that embraces both high and low
cultural interests.

The actors in Lali Chetwynd's performances are emphatically amateur. Through
chance encounters she has established a regular stable of performers, including a
carpenter, an IT specialist, an architect, a builder, a ceramicist, writers, painters,
musicians and buskers. Her performers are friends and acquaintances, people
willing to take part in something first and foremost as a favour to the artist. What
arises from performing together is the development of a group of relationships
that come from a shared experience.

Chetwynd in turn feeds off the different skills and sets of knowledge that each
individual performer brings – to the event and to her life in general. Club singers

Aelita, Queen of Mars,
2003
Post performance
production still
Kabinett der
Abstrakten, Bloomberg
SPACE, London

Anthropometry, 2002
Essor Project Space

found busking on the Underground provided the soundtrack to *Born Free*; musicians Chetwynd has met in bars provide the score and the live accompaniment; her father becomes Joy Adamson's husband; curators are given nappies to wear; writers don flesh-coloured body suits; and office workers make like the Hulk. There is no hierarchy when her homemade costumes are distributed.

Inspired by Levi-Strauss's *The Savage Mind*, Chetwynd sees herself as a *bricoleur*, using found materials and craft skills, constantly reusing materials and coming up with new solutions according to the ever-changing requirements of the job.

Chetwynd's subject matter is often about rehabilitating our knowledge and memory of characters that history has treated badly. By examining the unfashionable and using it as subject matter, she gives it new life. Meat Loaf has enjoyed a Chetwynd renaissance, as have bats, Yves Klein, the Hulk, Nero, pasta jewellery, and *Born Free*, the story of Elsa the lion and Joy Adamson.

Born Free was written by Joy Adamson in 1960 and reported the story of the rescue and rehabilitation of an orphaned lion cub. The book became a huge bestseller,

Born Free, 2004
Bloomberg New
Contemporaries,
Liverpool

bringing issues of wildlife conservation to an international audience. Joy Adamson was a strong and tyrannical woman, whose love for big cats far exceeded her affection for human beings; reports of her mistreatment of her employees were common. Chetwynd's performance, *Born Free, a Melodrama – The Death of a Conservationist*, dramatically portrays the events leading up to Adamson's death in 1980, when she was murdered by a worker with a grudge.

Lali Chetwynd's potentially difficult relationship with an audience asked to grapple with themes that are not immediately comprehensible has always been tempered by the good humour and generosity of her performances. Though often dealing with demanding and unfamiliar subjects, she approaches them with comedy, originality and passion for the people she performs with. Whether a performance makes sense immediately or not, the sight is enough to encourage the audience to ask for more, and Chetwynd's production of photocopied information, which often has a part in the event, supplies the spectators with some support. Unwittingly, the audience is drawn in, through astonishment, fascination, wit and sheer spectacle. For *Do Not Interrupt Your Activities*, Lali Chetwynd will be running *Pasta Necklace Workshop (Advance Classes in Bronze Age Jewellery),* where what is regarded as one of the lowest forms of 'art', often reserved for children, will be made available to all. Together the public will be able to construct jewellery and present it to The Discerning Eye, who will be played by Chetwynd's mother.

Sarah McCrory

Kim Coleman (b 1976) and Jenny Hogarth (b 1979)

Kim Coleman and Jenny Hogarth are hard to pin down. Their work spans an idiosyncratic range of subjects, embracing topics as diverse as the Venus de Milo and fireworks, corny popular imagery and four-hundred-year-old Scottish history, shadows and jelly. Their works span performance, film, sculpture and collage, and, as well as making work together, they collaborate with other people – sometimes dozens of other people – while also working as individuals. One of the consequences of this promiscuity of reference and practice is that it un-tethers objects and events from their original or designated meanings, letting them assume new symbolic and imaginative potential. Another is the pleasure of witnessing choreographed but makeshift spectacles in which artists and performers are clearly greatly enjoying themselves.

Employing home-spun materials, redundant technologies and ersatz bric-a-brac, many of Coleman and Hogarth's works have a lo-fi, retro appeal – the spectacular on the cheap, as it were. After graduating from Edinburgh College of Art in 2001, Coleman set up a gallery in her flat and made works that played off this domestic, intimate environment. *Untitled* (2002), a collaborative performance with Susie Green, 'remade, decelerated and reduced' a firework to an unpredictable progression of sparks and flares. Accompanied by music and watched by a small audience in a pitch-black room, its climax was an explosion of flashguns, bike lights and day-glo paint.

Kim Coleman and
Susie Green
Untitled, 2002
Photograph:
Hugh Watt

Kim Coleman
and Jenny Hogarth
*Who's the Greatest
Italian Painter?* 2004
Commissioned by
Babak Ghazi in
association with
Counter Gallery
Photograph:
Lucy Levine

In Coleman's *Kiss and Make-Up* (2004) hundreds of handmade slides were projected from multiple slide projectors onto a man's face, as though tears were streaming down his cheek – an artistic hybrid of performance and rudimentary animation. Other works by Coleman exploit the drama inherent in shadows as well as light projection. Collaborating in April last year with Dave Maclean at the VSF (Vacant Shop Front) gallery in Glasgow, *Amazing Grace* took the form of shadow silhouettes, rendering a saucy fairytale in subverted symmetry against a sharp back light. A collage by Coleman entitled *Amaryllis sillyramA* (2004) takes this theme of screwed symmetry and distorted reflection further and spells it out. An amaryllis is a lily-like flower and also the name for a shepherdess or country girl in pastoral poetry. And the title, of course, is a palindrome, a reflection that flips between the poetic and the goofy, the pastoral bucolic and the confected poptastic. Against a silhouetted landscape, the collage combines the symmetry of swans with necks locked in sentimental embrace with the instantly sinister shape of a mushroom cloud. Like the title, the work flips between wildly discordant tenors of collective recognition.

Hogarth's work is similarly full of odd contrasts, incongruities and distorted reflections. In *This Is Not A Fashion Parade* (2004), a filmed performance, she and Coleman are bizarrely kitted out in old-fashioned, full-skirted ball dresses, waltzing their way together down a ski-slope on snowboards. This mini love story is accompanied by a wistful song, but it is the incongruousness of their activity that makes it touching: their hands-holding togetherness, as much as their billowing skirts, is a rare sight on the ski-slopes, and they clearly have to trust each other much more than they would on the dance floor. *Gelatine Figurine* (2003), a fifteen

Jenny Hogarth
Pentland Rising, 2004
Collage, Commissioned
by Collective Gallery

centimetre high Venus de Milo made out of translucent edible jelly and residing slumped in a fridge, represents another marriage of mis-matched elements. By reconstituting her in jelly, Hogarth gave the Venus a more empathetic aspect. She looks, according to Hogarth, 'drunk and sleepy and sort of in a huff ... a truculent look conveying the modern woman.'

In other works Hogarth re-drafts famous historical events, which, like the *Gelatine Figurine,* recast the original in an altogether different scale, tone and location. *Pentland Rising* (2004), a re-enactment of crucial and bloody moments in Scottish history, took place, for no discernable reason, on a dry-ski slope. Unlike Jeremy Deller's *The Battle of Orgreave*, which strove to re-awaken all the original emotion in its restaging, Hogarth's re-enactment is a fabulously choreographed romp, incorporating music, lights and compere and dozens of costumed skiers. Rather than attempting to re-stage history, Hogarth's re-enactment referenced other re-enactments – those hackneyed pageants that, whether civic or Disney, ritually repeat their own clichés. Occurring during the Edinburgh Festival, *Pentland Rising* can be seen as an artistic extension of the Military Tattoo and Festival Fireworks.

This kind of burlesque is typical of Hogarth and Coleman's practice, which borrows from leisure activities, gala displays, amateur dramatics and choreographed pyrotechnics. Referencing entertainment rather than art history or art discourse, and refusing to take themselves too seriously, her performances bring people together for an experience of extrovert celebration.

Gair Boase

Robin Deacon (b 1973)

Robin Deacon's work invites us to think about racial politics, using highly intelligent, anarchic humour. With a combination of slapstick comedy and what appears to be barely contained rage, his lecture performances are profoundly unsettling. In his recent performed lectures, *Harry and Me* (2004) and *Colin Powell* (2004), he assumes the semi-autobiographical persona of a conspiracy theorist, inventing multiple layers of the character Robin Deacon.

In *Harry and Me*, Deacon investigates the circumstances surrounding his childhood appearance, as a member of his Bedford school choir, in Harry Secombe's religious television programme *Highway*. Deacon revisits the controversy that surrounded this innocent seeming event. It was rumoured that the 'ethnic' children had been planted in the choir to provide the racially integrated image of Bedford required by the programme's producers.

In the performance, Deacon recounts his quest to find television footage of the show in order to discover why he was really asked to join the choir just a few weeks before the event. Was it thinly-veiled tokenism? Can Deacon even sing? Deacon gives his lecture on the case wearing his old school uniform and solemnly presenting the facts on a projector. Supporting evidence is carefully examined including local newspaper coverage from the time and Deacon's old school reports which praise his amenable nature. Deacon treats his serious subject matter with a beguiling combination of anger and humour. He hints, however, that perhaps his recollections are not to be trusted. Could his theory be paranoid fantasy? Deacon is hard to pin down. He keeps the audience guessing as to which, if any, of his delivered opinions are his own.

In his satirical monologue *Colin Powell*, Deacon compares his own life to that of Colin Powell. Throughout the performance, Deacon stands with his back to the audience, claiming that he bears an uncanny resemblance to Colin Powell as he proceeds to deconstruct the American politician's public image. It eventually transpires that Deacon only looks like Powell in so far as he has the same skin colour. Weaving in tales from his past, Deacon playfully exploits the clichés of performance art: smearing food substances on his skin and urinating and convulsing on stage.

During the lecture, Deacon dissects Powell's ambivalent reception by the black community. Here is a black man who achieved a position of power in a

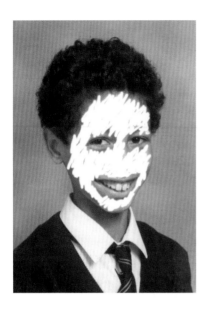

Photograph
manipulated
by Robin Deacon
Courtesy of the artist

predominantly white political establishment but, as an ultraconservative, absorbed rather than challenged prevailing value systems. Deacon draws comparisons with his own formative experiences. He tells us that he was deeply unpopular amongst black children, who accused him of betraying his so-called roots because he didn't like rap music. Deacon quotes Harry Belafonte, who derided Powell as a 'house slave', one who has the privilege of living in the master's house because he serves the master exactly as he wants to be served. Deacon draws parallels between a photograph of the young Powell shaking hands with Nixon, and his own souvenir photo recording him receiving a 'Debenhams Employee of the Month Award' from his manager. This is hilarious and shocking because the juxtaposition is so absurd, and yet so apt.

One of Deacon's ongoing projects is an exploration of notions of obscenity. For his video *Passionate About* (2001), a single text was created by weaving together a profanity-strewn piece of 'gangsta rap' describing sexual violence towards women and an article from *Railway Modeller* magazine, describing the joy derived from a model steam train. These contradictory texts are cut up and shuffled, like an exquisite corpse, with the hybrid text becoming the script of the video. There is an

Colin Powell, 2004–5
Photograph:
Mira Vogel, 2003
Courtesy of the artist

uncomfortable discord between tones and view points and we are not sure which text we are hearing. Deacon is interested in those areas where the vocabulary of the texts overlaps, but with wildly different contexts.

Deacon applied the same technique in *Let's Talk About Racism* (2001–2002). A children's advice book on racism is spliced with Robert Crumb's *When the Niggers Take Over America,* itself a caustic satire on US culture. Deacon revels in playing with our expectations of genre and context.

The Costello Show (1999–2001) is a re-enactment of an Elvis Costello press conference in which the singer attempted to vindicate himself after using the word 'nigger'. Costello's squirming efforts to defend himself against charges of racism, which become increasingly desperate and unconvincing, are hilariously performed by Deacon.

Deacon often muses on the place of humour in performance art. In his performances and his writing, he interrogates the po-faced performance art clichés of self-harm, angst, nudity, the use of bodily fluids and protracted duration. His live work is fast-paced and witty, cerebral and self-critical. He admits: 'Granted, certain items of clothing are often removed during my performances, but I always endeavour to do this in an amusing manner'. Deacon is interested in the mechanics of humour. For him, laughter is an aggressive act in the antagonistic relationship between artist and audience. He wants his audience to laugh and then to regret that they laughed.

Ali MacGilp

Richard Dedomenici (b 1978)

Richard Dedomenici's lecture performance, *Embracing Failure* (2004), takes the audience on a whirlwind tour of his 'less successful' performance projects. This cathartic enterprise provides a detailed compendium of his practice: a series of futile acts and subtle interventions in his immediate environment. Often governed by chance, his exploits of mild civil disobedience are removed from the gallery space, aiming to engage directly with an unsuspecting, and sometimes unwilling, audience of passers-by.

Despite his claims to undermine current political, social and corporate structures, Dedomenici's projects are harmless. Regardless, he audaciously manipulates a variety of issues that affect our daily lives. He claims that his actions are 'primarily dedicated to the development and implementation of innovative strategies designed to undermine accepted belief systems and topple existing powers'[1]. *Party of One* (2001) commissioned by Chapter Arts Centre, Cardiff, was an early example of his attempt to challenge these structures. Provoked by British Telecom's announcement that they were to stop expanding their telephone box network, *Party of One* was a futile attempt to increase the use of public phone boxes, despite the mobile phone industry showing no obvious sign of collapse. To achieve his pledge, Dedomenici spent the day blowing up balloons in a cluster of phone boxes, until there was no room left. Knowing the attention his clowning would attract, he placed in the neighbouring boxes call cards in the style of those distributed by prostitutes. 'I like rubber', they read, 'I'll blow up balloons as you watch'. Phoning the number on the card provided callers with the answer as to what this strange man was up to. Some, however, took the cards to be the genuine article and tried to initiate a sexually explicit *tête à tête*. By whatever means, Dedominici increased the number of calls and fulfilled his pledge, albeit momentarily.

Encouraged by his tutor to test the boundaries of his medium, Dedomenici attempted the performance *Break-in* (2001) which resulted in his being escorted away by the police. A half-hearted attempt to scale the walls of Cardiff Prison, *Break-in* was not well received by the authorities, although the artist never passed the 3ft mark. Handcuffed and tired from the hard work, Dedomenici managed to persuade the bemused policeman that it was a harmless work of art and he was eventually released. 'Ever since a teacher promised me a good mark for a performance piece if I got arrested, I have been pretty good at getting out of trouble by claiming that what I am doing is art.'[2]

1 www.dedomenici.co.uk
2 Rhodri Marsden, The Guardian, Monday, January 17, 2005

Employing a lunatic humour as his secret weapon, Dedomenici often targets the current political scene. The playful nature of his performances allows him to tackle sensitive issues. His most recent works have probed the nation's paranoia about terrorist attacks, ridiculing our fears under the pretence of serious concern. As part of his one-month residency at the Edinburgh Fringe Festival, *HMS Belfast* (2003) highlighted the possible hijacking of the popular tourist attraction anchored in the river Thames. Dedomenici proposed moving the primary gun turrets of this naval relic so that they pointed towards his mother's house on the outskirts of London, where he lives. 'In these times of heightened security I was at first unnerved to discover that such a powerful weapon was parked in the middle of London. The fact that I am willing to target it at my place of residence is a testament to the safety measures in place'[3]. Unfortunately the event was cancelled at the last minute, but

Boris, 2004
Commissioned by
Bluecoat for
Liverpool Biennial
Streets of Liverpool
Courtesy of the artist

3 Richard Dedomenici, HMS Belfast, July 2003

this did not discourage Dedomenici from continuing his campaign to reinforce safety measures and to reveal further possible terrorist strategies. In August 2003 he presented *Sexed-Up, a study into the potential threat posed by Weapons of Mass Destruction lying dormant in our midst*. On this occasion the artist centred his concerns on the possibility of blowing up the Scottish Parliament Building at Holyrood, Edinburgh, which stands in the line of fire of the iron cannon housed at Edinburgh Castle.

Making people laugh is vital to the success of Dedominici's projects. Often conveyed to a wider audience through newspaper articles and TV reports, his practice verges on more mainstream modes of entertainment. In October 2004, as part of the Liverpool Biennial, he decided to dress up as the Tory MP Boris Johnson and offered Liverpudlians their long awaited apology, following Johnson's accusation that the city was wallowing in self-pity after the tragic execution of Ken Bigley by Iraqi rebels. The Tory MP's comment caused anger among a community that had united to campaign for Bigley's release. Dedomenici, in a foolish disguise assembled from charity shop purchases and well placed plasters, took to the streets of Liverpool. Offering his hand and placing apologetic stickers on lapels, he appropriated the prankish strategies of comic entertainment. Once again, he escaped unscathed.

Gulf Sale, 2004
Streets of London
Photograph:
Luci Briginshaw

Dedomenici's ephemeral deeds seldom attract success. Always dependent on the response of an improvised audience of passers-by, he initiates situations over which he seems to have very little control. Despite his claims, these actions actually have no predetermined conclusion but they test situations and the responses of those who are unwittingly involved. The fascination of his work lies in his stubborn belief in his endeavours, rather than in their outcomes.

Carmen Juliá and Cassandra Needham

Quit Your Flappin',
2004, Chicago
Courtesy of the artist

Harrell Fletcher (b 1967)

Harrell Fletcher takes images and stories from individuals, as well as from literature, as material for research into the human condition. Driven by his own interests, Fletcher often acts as director, giving assignments, asking people to reveal personal knowledge and memories. In February 2005, I met with Harrell to find out more about the ideas that guide his work.

LD: Which artists have influenced your practice?

HF: I come primarily from a photography background, so I was looking at a lot of photographers' work: Robert Frank, Nancy Rexroth, Wendy Ewald, Robert Adams, Larry Sultan, Jim Goldberg, John Gossage. Wendy Ewald's book *Portraits and Dreams* was possibly the single most influential thing I came across. It's about her work with kids in a rural part of Kentucky. I was also very interested in documentary films, especially ones made by non-traditional film makers like George Kuchar, The Maysles Brothers, Chantal Akerman, Ross McElwee. In addition I was interested in non-fiction writers like Joan Didion, Anne Dillard, V.S Naipaul, and Calvin Trillin. And I was very influenced early on by the comic book *American Splendor* by Harvey Pekar. I wanted to see how I could adapt the kind of content and style I was seeing in all of that work into a visual art context, galleries, museums, and public art. That might seem like a strange thing to want to do, but somehow I had wound up being trained as a visual artist, in some ways by default, and it seemed like the thing for me to do was make my interests work in that arena.

LD: Do you see your Ideas, assignments you have posted on your website of activities to be completed by individuals, in the same lineage as 1960s conceptual work like Lawrence Weiner's instruction pieces? What attitude, if any, does your work share with the 1960s DIY work?

HF: The 60s conceptual stuff often gets mentioned as a possible influence of mine, and I'm sure in some ways it was, but when I initially found out about it I wasn't very excited by it, and I rarely thought about it directly. It seemed too dry, and too self-contained within the art world. It was always about making art, and I'm not interested in making art for the most part. I'm interested in finding ways to engage with life. Maybe those conceptualists would say the same thing, but that wasn't the feeling I got.

LD: Who, outside of the arts, has influenced your practice and how?

HF: Besides all of the people I mentioned before who I was interested in not only in terms of content but also in style, I was also really interested in other writers more purely because of what they had to say, not so much how they said it. Some of those books and writers are *Summerhill* by A.S Neill, *The Good Life* by Helen and Scott Nearning, *The No-Work Garden Book* by Ruth Stout, *How Children Learn* by John Holt, *Savage Inequalities* by Jonathan Kozol. Actually, I really like all of those people's writing styles too, but the content was particularly compelling to me. I think I was also very influenced by a five-year-old boy named Walter that I worked with in an after-school program when I was in my early twenties. I taught Walter how to make books and he started making a different one every day, showing them to as many people as he could and then basically discarding them, but I kept several of them. Another huge influence was working at Creativity Explored which is an art studio for developmentally disabled adults in San Francisco. The people I met and worked with there completely turned my world around in a really good way. I consider both Walter and the Creativity Explored folks artists though, so they sort of fell into the wrong question here.

LD: Your video work is strongly connected to your live collaborative events. For both, you incorporate real people's narratives as well as strong literary references. Could you tell me about how you came to The Problem of Possible Redemption?

HF: First I made *Blot Out The Sun* which was done in Portland, Oregon at a gas station. I'd heard the owner Jay Dykman wanted a movie made there so I went and

Yellow Dancing Kids, 2004, Lamda print and latex paint Courtesy of the Artist

asked him if I could help him do it. He was really excited, but wanted me to do the whole thing – he just wanted it to happen there. I asked him to at least give me some direction on what he had in mind and he told me that he thought it should be like *Ulysses*, by James Joyce. I thought that was pretty great so I went off and bought a copy and started reading it. Then I got so into the book that I decided that I would just use lines from it and have people at the gas station read them off of cue cards. We shot and edited the whole movie in about three weeks and then screened it at night at the gas station. All of the participants came to see themselves. So that went well. Then I was doing a project in Hartford, Connecticut in this neighborhood called Parkville. I knew I wanted to include the senior center that was there in some part of the project and I thought I could use the same structure of taking lines from a suggested book, but no one there had any suggestions, so I just decided to use *Ulysses* again. I could probably do ten or twenty different videos using different lines from *Ulysses*, it just has so much going on in it. So I created a new script of cue cards and this time focused primarily on one actor, this senior named Walter Cutler. I sort of tailored the script to him. It was a lot about dealing with mortality, and sort of ethical questions that you face when you are alive. In that case too the first screening was there on site in front of the Senior Center.

LD: How do you describe your role in the organization of participants in live events?

The Sound We Make Together,
2003, Performed
at Diverseworks
Courtesy of the Artist

HF: I work with people in a variety of roles, sometimes assistant, sometime collaborator, sometimes facilitator, sometimes director, sometimes friend, sometimes editor, but really I don't think in those terms, I'm just doing the work that I want to do with the people I want to work with and hoping that everyone has a positive experience.

LD: Tell me more about the lecture event, Come Together (London), that you are organizing for our exhibition?

HF: The *Come Together* event is about trying to bring together a selection of people who have something to share with each other but might not have an outlet for that sharing, or the outlet might be very exclusive. I want the knowledge to be made available to a wider audience. I'm doing a slightly different version in Austin and will call it *What We Talk About*, a reference to the Raymond Carver book *What We Talk About When We Talk About Love*.

LD: Do you feel that in relation to the current political situation in the US your work is creating a utopia, a small revolution?

HF: Not a utopia, I'm too much of a realist to make a claim like that. Maybe it's a utopian event, or a smallish revolt, or just a coming together. I don't know. I just wanted to harness the energy that exists when people get together for a party or an opening or something like that and make it more functional and instructional. It's like a way to skip over small talk and get on to the big talk that everyone has within them, but is not often encouraged to come out. Also, I wanted to make a space where people felt welcome and where they could share the spotlight, rather than just coming to be an audience for one speaker or one band or one person's art.

LD: What was your favorite moment at Come Together (New York) at Apex Art, New York on 12 February 2005?

HF: I like the group meditation and physical activities. I tend to be a little stressed out all the time, so it's nice to incorporate a little relaxation into my work.

LD: What specifically are you hoping will happen with Come Together (London) at the Royal College of Art on 9 April 2005?

HF: That we will learn some stuff from each other, and that we will have fun, and maybe feel a little sense of hope about the future of this world. I've been feeling really depressed about this Bush situation and I need to create things that take me out of my bleakness. These events really help.

Lillian Davies

David Hatcher (b 1973)

David Hatcher's work reduces thought systems and philosophical discourses to the simplest of forms. He not only plays with art historical discourses but simultaneously interrogates the mechanisms that shape our social, political and economic structures. In this conversation with David Hatcher, I try to unravel a few of those strands.

CN: I would like to start off with *Holding Pattern*, the first piece you made that incorporated directly quoted texts. Could you tell me how this work came about?

DH: In February 1998 the New Zealand government sent a booklet called 'Towards a code of Social and Family Responsibility' to all New Zealand households. It was very bleak, even for unsolicited mail. Tucked away on the last page was an imprint identifying the publisher as the Corporate Communications Unit of the Department of Social Welfare. I decided to engrave the eleven 'expectations' out of that publication into fake marble plaques. I thought of them as mobile inscriptions, the kind of work that might make sense in any of the welfare states of the overdeveloped world that were being dismantled. The government seemed to be reconstituting itself as a service provider, nothing more. The implications for the ideals I'd grown up with were breathtaking, though not of course unique to New Zealand. The

Oedipal Manoeuvres in the Dark
Flourescent pigment and acrylic on wall
Installation view: müllerdechiara, Berlin, 2005
Photo: Ludger Paffrath
Courtesy of müllerdechiara, Berlin

People will do all they can to keep themselves physically and mentally healthy.

expectations' that appear as verbatim quotes in *Holding Pattern* are the noxious fruit of free market ideals. They are however simply one national instance of a strain of thinking ascendant internationally at the time. The ghosts of earlier forms of state coercion inhabit these statements. If there is a non-sequitur here, it is because, despite superficial affinities to historical forms of government that embodied Christian or Socialist ideologies, these are statements disseminated by a secular, capitalist state apparatus. I briefly considered substituting all instances of the word 'people' with 'artists', but decided that somebody encountering the work might register these sorts of associations without further coercion on my part. I was very interested in the paradox of presenting all this in a gallery context, cross-pollinating art historical and political notions of representation.

CN: I'd like to know more about the role of this paradox of representation in your practice. You have incorporated art historical and political references into a number of projects – I'm thinking particularly of the ongoing *Twenty-twenty-twenty* series in which you remix historical statements from the twentieth century into objects that resemble eye charts. What considerations guide your selection of texts in that series, how do you arrive at these specific citations?

DH: I started with André Breton and recently I've been working with Kate Sheppard, Adam Smith, Angela Davis, the Ramones, Ian Burn. The text samples are not necessarily attributable to individuals, though most of them are. They're also not necessarily immediately associated with art or universalist, utopian projects. But they're all affiliated with certain positions or postures in politics, economics, art history etc. And they all had a certain influence on, or represented, something that peaked in the twentieth century. And then they've had an impact on me as well, a direct impact. So this project is a self-portrait, but it's also a monument to a kind of positional vertigo that typifies twentieth-century subjectivity in the West. It was a century of what might these days be referred to as hard landings for notions of the

Holding Pattern, 1998
11 Engraved acrylic plaques
Dimensions variable, each *c*. 7 × 18 cm
Collection Charlotte Armstrong and Anthony Drumm, Berlin

self that emerged from the Enlightenment. The manner in which such positions are optically indexed in that series makes them appear more or less indistinguishable from each other.

CN: In *Oedipal Manoeuvres in the Dark* you seem to be challenging the knowledge of the gallery audience. You appropriate diagrams deployed to illustrate Western philosophical texts but you eliminate all the descriptive labels and thereby to some extent their context. Could you explain the motivation behind this process and your relationship to the canonical texts you are sourcing these images from?

DH: *Oedipal Manoeuvres in the Dark* surveys ideas or concepts that contributed to the constitution of the Western Bloc. Notions of social or political agency, free will, definitions of good, evil or love, that sort of thing. But it does this at what seems like an exclusively formal level, through the most 'authentic' visual representations of those ideas that exist – the diagrams or figures that their authors composed or commissioned as visual complements to their writing. After I started archiving diagrams and schemas from the pages of philosophy books I decided the textual appendages were less interesting than the actual shapes themselves, and what I found most intriguing about these forms was repetition and abstraction. A proliferation of circles, triangles and squares, for the most part. While these shapes often index ideas or positions that are irreconcilable, assumptions about absolute categories or classes of objects and subjects are not challenged. They tend to illustrate universals, and those universals are often in conflict with each other. There's a lot of naïve set theory involved in such visual formalisation of concepts. You could say there's a lot of naïve set theory underpinning a lot of the concepts themselves. I'm very interested in the relationship between that and, say, modernist abstraction in the visual arts. There's a lot of categorical thinking there too. What's probably most interesting about this to artists is the role of the exception in all this. What happens to the subject or object that doesn't fit into these constructed categories or classes? Adam Smith is quite clear about this: an individual who can no longer subsist within a free market structure must, for the greater good, be 'allowed to die'. Such systemic violence is implicit in the fine print of today's liberal secular societies. Joey Ramone puts it like this: 'if you're not in it, you're out of it'. All this started off as an investigation of forms in books I carried with me when I travelled, but then I decided to go to libraries and get more comprehensive about it.

There's always that idea that artists only look at the pictures when they read books anyway, so if you did that to the history of Western philosophy, this is the kind of occult knowledge you might acquire. I'm not sure how Hegel, Kant, Schopenhauer,

Ludwig and Hugh,
2004
Flourescent pigment
on wall, 183 × 279 cm
Studio view, UCLA,
Los Angeles
Photograph: Gene Ogami
Courtesy of Starkwhite,
Auckland

Bergson or Badiou would feel about seeing their compositions represented in fluorescent pigment on a wall like this. In a sense I'm poking fun at a kind of critical endgame here.

CN: *Oedipal Manoeuvres in the Dark* addresses aspects of philosophical discourse much more literally than earlier works – it seems that the position of the individual within a broader schema is still an integral part of your practice. How does this relate to earlier pieces like *Holding Pattern*?

DH: *Holding Pattern* seems as concrete to me as *Oedipal Manoeuvres in the Dark*. These works share a cranked up identification with authority and an interest in coercion. With *Holding Pattern* the coercive attempts of the state to influence the behaviour of individuals are rendered as blank mimicry. *Oedipal Manoeuvres in the Dark* pays more attention to certain modalities of intellectual practice that underwrote the creation of the nation states of modernity. There's something fanatical about all this. Both works display an interest in the legacy of conceptual practices in the visual arts, and relationships between political or philosophical discourses and aesthetics. In their own ways, they're both attempts to negotiate the burden of those histories. Without the philosophical genealogies that *Oedipal Manoeuvres in the Dark* surveys there wouldn't be any liberal secular ideologies for something like *Holding Pattern* to parody. In both pieces the individual, in this case the kind of person who frequents contemporary art galleries, is triangulated in relation to the political, philosophical and art historical traditions that these works invoke.

CN: Do you see *Holding Pattern* as highlighting a rupture between visual arts

practice and political or philosophical discourse? You appear at times to be questioning the artwork's power to reach an audience beyond the exhibition context. Are you demonstrating a disbelief in the artist's ability to engage a wider audience when such issues are presented solely within the format of an exhibition?

DH: I think it totally depends on the exhibition, but yes, I want to acknowledge the limits of the generic exhibition context. I don't think this should be lamented. I'm not idealistic about galleries as sites for the presentation of contemporary art. For some people galleries and museums are social clubs, for some they're chapels, or they've replaced chapels. Others see them as social laboratories, boutiques, clinics or sites for entertainment or edification. At various times they might be all of these. Of course artists are able to engage with broader audiences and communities through their work, but the representation of such interventions in a traditional exhibition context should not be confused with such acts, gestures or projects themselves. In some cases, the representation of the latter in a gallery environment is antithetical to the kind of engagement you're referring to. A sort of capitulation. The interesting question here for me is that of constituency. With whom is the artist attempting to establish or sustain relationships? Adorno said that to say 'we' but mean 'I' is the most recondite of insults.

CN: So there is a risk that presenting acts of engagement within the gallery kills the work's gesture? Is there a degree of cynicism here about the extent to which an art object can appeal for direct action? Or are you more concerned about the limits of an artist's ability to be critical about the social, political and economic systems in which they themselves operate?

DH: It's not cynicism, but I'm pragmatic about this. What is the efficacy of a critical visual arts practice today? Can we even speak of something like this? For a start, when people use the word 'art' they're not necessarily referring to the same thing. What is interesting to me about what Bourriaud refers to as 'operational realism' is its limit. Could parts of the Second Surrealist Manifesto incite indiscriminate murder? Possibly, but it is important to remember that Breton is taunting his readers by saying that if they can't *imagine* dashing into a street and firing a pistol blindly into a crowd, they deserve to be in that crowd ready to be shot by somebody who can. This sounds pretty antagonistic doesn't it, but how many Surrealists actually went postal?

Cassandra Needham

Emily Jacir (b 1970)

Emily Jacir's practice is directly linked to the restricted freedom of movement inflicted on Palestinians since the imposition of new frontiers and increasingly severe control on border crossings between Palestine and the state of Israel. Her work is not based around historical facts or political debates however, but focuses on the individual's experience of grief and dissatisfaction when this lack of a homeland, or lack of liberty, manifests itself as the impossibility of free action in everyday life.

Identifying the consequences of displacement in individuals, Jacir evidences a need to focus on ordinary people's lives and to understand the real effects of political conflicts – it seems there is not much likelihood we can thoroughly appreciate the reality of the situation historically or via the press. Jacir's works choose people, not systems, and at the same time expose the existence of a displaced community of people who suffer from the same discomfort. Her work usually presents an over-whelming accumulation of similar personal situations, manifesting the magnitude and extent of the consequences of exile.

The restrictions on freedom are highlighted by the existence of a parallel liberty that others experience. Jacir herself enacts this difference: she is a Palestinian

Sexy Semite,
2000–2002
Photograph:
O.K. Books, Courtesy
of Anthony Reyolds
Gallery, London

Sexy Semite,
2000–2002
Personal ads placed
in the *Village Voice*
Courtesy of the
Anthony Reynolds
Gallery

holder of a US Passport who can move freely across borders, although this becomes
more and more difficult as time goes by. She makes use of her more fortunate
situation to perform and represent the transits banned or made very difficult
for others.

For *Where We Come From* (2001–2003) Jacir offered to carry out tasks for
Palestinians from around the world in a land they could not enter due to psycho-
logical barriers or to the nature of their ID. She asked 'If I could do anything for you,
anywhere in Palestine, what would it be?'. She got answers as varied as 'Go to
Bayt Lahia and bring me a photo of my family, especially my brother's kids' or 'Go to
the Israeli Post Office in Jerusalem and pay my phone bill'. Jacir carried out these
petitions, these expressions of longing, and documented each of them with a
photograph or a film. She later exhibited the text of the request with the person's
reason for not being able to execute it and a photograph in which we can see
her performing the task. Poetic and powerful, her work attempts to fulfil these
people's wishes but does not try to solve the problem presented. In Jacir's work
there is an assumption that things cannot be changed easily. Exile seems incurable.
Nevertheless, she is clearly denouncing the barriers these people are facing;
empathy is successfully targeted to make the audience aware of the situation.

The condition of exile is also highlighted in Jacir's *Sexy Semite* (2000–2002), an
intervention in the *Village Voice* newspaper where she had friends publish mock
ads searching for Jewish mates in the Personals section. This piece employs a starkly
different register to *Where We Come From*. Over the course of three years, ads
appeared with texts such as 'You stole the Land, may as well take the Women!

Where We Come From (Jihad), 2001–2003
Framed laser print
and c-print mounted
on cintra, Courtesy of
Anthony Reynolds
Gallery

Redhead Palestinian ready to be colonized by your army' or 'Palestinian Semite in search of Jewish soul mate. Do you love milk & honey? I'm ready to start a big family in Israel. Still have house keys. Waiting for you'. The ads caused surprise and, especially after 2001, alarmed the press, who covered the news of the 'infiltration' considering the ads might be a terrorist alert.

Time plays a major part in Jacir's work. Past, present and future mingle in her approach to exile and movement. Jacir's work remembers the past, declares the reality of the present and imagines a different future as a strategy to cope with the burden of exile and uncertainty. She somehow heals the lack of place with the creation of a new space, a space of hope. While rooted in a displaced land, her work acts as a site for resistance and as a medium to express the desire to do what is out of reach and to present the instability of a life in exile. As an artist, Jacir makes the most of the symbolic power of art – and the possibilities offered by its system – to produce a place from which a vital testimony of the present can be presented and a history constructed.

Alejandra Aguado

Jesper Just (b 1974)

Immured in a mahogany-clad Gentleman's club a silver-haired man, dusty with age, waits at a table-for-one for a telephone call. A telephone rings. The man lifts his receiver. The telephone continues to ring until it is answered by another silver-haired man. The man looks around expectantly, almost defeated by his telephone. The camera angles out, revealing a room filled with similar men – all silver-haired, stiff, and expectant. They are caged by a dappled light which pours down upon them and are surrounded by a small army of menacing black standard lights and portraits that stare. They are awkward denizens, resting nervously, in the almost-dark.

A directed finger moves towards the dial on a telephone. It dials a number and the telephone rings out. The silver-haired man is suddenly consumed by an unnatural pool of light as the camera rushes towards him. This shot is followed by a close-up of a young man's mouth – his lips puckered and glistening. The telephone is answered by the old man and a pregnant silence ensues. The silence is broken by the young man, played by actor Johannes Lilleøre, who begins to sing Big Band crooner, Horace Heidt's *I Don't Want to Set the World on Fire*:

> *I don't want to set the world on fire*
> *I just want to start*
> *A flame in your heart*
> *In my heart I have but one desire*
> *And that one is you*
> *No other will do*

The older man responds with a verse from *Address Unknown,* first performed by the Ink Spots in 1939:

> *Address unknown – not even a trace of you.*
> *Oh what I'd give to see the face of you.*
> *I was a fool to stay away from you so long.*
> *I should have known there'd come a day when you'd be gone.*

The odd-couple continue their duet, until the old man is left alone, singing into a receiver which has been abandoned.

Making explicit references to the film oeuvre of David Lynch, *The Lonely Villa*, with its deliberate and lackadaisical pacing, hung off a score which seems to thicken and

The Lonely Villa, 2004
16mm film transferred
to video, 5 min 30 sec
Courtesy of Perry
Rubenstein Gallery,
New York

Image courtesy of
Galleri Christina
Wilson, Copenhagen
and Perry Rubenstein
Gallery, New York

No Man Is An Island II,
2004, 4 min.
Courtesy of the artist
and Perry Rubenstein
Gallery, New York

deepen around the characters as the film persists, suggests a cigar-stained dream state. Jesper Just gives the very real desire of one man to touch the life of another a make-believe setting and and then stops before anything concrete can be declared. Where does fantasy end and reality begin?

The Lonely Villa is littered with allusions to David Lynch, from the use of spotlights to highlight elements of the mise-en-scene, and the pools of light cast by standard lamps, to the camera close-ups on mouths. Just's cinephiliac embrace raises questions about the position of his films in the context of the gallery. His work seems to oppose the prevalent trend in contemporary art-film production, which has recently privileged the documentary-turn. Just's high production values, his insistence on working with trained actors, composers, sound engineers and singers, and his commitment to acting as both director and editor stand in stark contrast to the low-fi aesthetic and its accompanying set of ethical rules pursued by a slew of other young artists working today with this medium. By abstracting both his 'activity' as an artist and the activities of his protagonists, and filtering them through an idiosyncratic language of cinematic history, does Just engage with the current argument about the capacity of video work to 'document' reality? Or is it that Just's work, so heavily indebted to Lynch, Elia Kazan, Bob Fosse and Lars von Trier, should be seen from the film-historical perspective and understood as a form of appropriational art?

Just consciously plays on the idea of video art as a construct that can verge on the real through the creation of fictions and the picturing of other worlds. Just is not merely flirting with cinematic clichés, instead he is playing with the presumptions of falsity that usually accompany filmic cultural transmissions, deftly exploiting the shady commerce between art and truth.

The Lonely Villa is about the ability of one individual to act upon another, but Just chooses to mediate this act not only through the medium of film, but also through a film which is essentially about other films. By abstracting and detaching the human act to such an extent, Just poses questions about the possibility of human action outside the surreal space of cinema, interrogating the possible 'realities' in which an act might take place.

James Lindon

Leopold Kessler

Disguised in a janitor's blue coat and armed with a silver toolbox, Leopold Kessler subtly alters civic property or makes unofficial repairs to public services. His interventions in public space are actions that correct an urban problem or that alter the social meaning of a particular situation. For this exhibition Kessler has installed locks in various telephone boxes throughout London. Videos of his interventions are shown in the gallery space.

AM: What is it that interests you in making these changes in our environment?

LK: Public space is naturally a restricted area, as people have to be coordinated – it's a very complex system of power and individual intentions. The anonymity of public space gives me the possibility of acting unnoticed, as people only react if your actions conform to some idea of criminal behaviour. I'm interested in this tension between individual freedom, egoism and the interests of the authorities who have to maintain public order.

AM: It seems to me you are trying to make citizens question their relationship to their environment – through an empowerment, by increasing the degree of access to public space, but also through questioning whether or not that access was already there to begin with.

Privatized,
2001–2003
Photographs of
intervention
Courtesy of the artist
and Corentin Hamel
Gallery, Paris

*'I installed receiver into eight streetlamps which enable me
to switch the lamps on/off by a remote control.'*

LK: If you introduce a strange object into public space most people will think 'this is art' and stop wondering about it, because they have an explanation for it. That's why I'm trying to install devices that seem to follow the logic of municipal authorities at first sight. Therefore it's important that they have an 'official' look. The locks that I install in the phone boxes pick upon a currently very fashionable topic: security. Authorities legitimize restrictions through the argument of protecting 'us' against potential dangers. To make people follow your instructions, you just have to make them afraid. The project with the locks taps into that: a lock means protection, but it also raises the question of against whom and what.

AM: Many of your projects – the intercom on the public tannoy system, the locks in the telephone boxes or the remote controls for streetlights – invert notions of public and private. To what degree do you feel you are giving citizens a new responsibility for their city and what about the potential for negative outcomes?

LK: In the case of the intercom the potential for misuse is a crucial point. The intercom gives you a power you know you shouldn't have. It's not just something like a speaker's corner, you speak through an official channel as the project involves a loudspeaker used for announcements by the public transport system. This power, as it has the potential for misuse, makes you behave more responsibly I believe.

AM: But the intercom could be used to assemble a riot or some kind of disturbance?

LK: The intercom project was installed a year ago and I showed the video twice in exhibitions in Vienna, so a lot of people know about it. If misuse had happened to occur, the secret would have been revealed, people would have reported it and the authorities would have banned access. When you use the intercom, you are more or less hidden, but you see the people you are speaking to; they are not abstract. I think anonymity is often a condition for misuse. The telephone locks function the other way around, don't they? You can only lock yourself in, not others, but the potential for misuse is still in one's imagination. The lock is there for protection – but what if a bad guy wants to protect himself?

AM: Are you keeping an eye on how your projects are used?

LK: This is difficult. Most of my interventions are designed to last for a long time and are used rarely. I cannot keep an eye on them even for two weeks; I'm not patient enough for this.

AM: Regarding the specificity of your interventions, do you try to locate your projects across the spectrum of the city's different areas to address a potential spectrum of use?

Secured, 2005
Video of intervention
Commissioned on
the occasion of the
*Do Not Interrupt
Your Activities*
Courtesy of the artist
and Corentin Hamel
Gallery, Paris

LK: I try to avoid working for specific groups of society. Laws are the same for all citizens (at least in theory) so, if an intervention can be realized in an edition (this depends on cost and effort) I like to spread it out. The locks for example are installed in different neighborhoods. When I show the documentation of these interventions in a gallery space subtle differences may become apparent. Here you may ask yourself about all the different ways in which you as a passer-by (depending on your personal inhibitions) might have been tempted to interact. The imagining of these possibilities comes from showing the projects in the gallery space.

AM: So the art context literally adds another perspective to your projects. Would you describe your work then as being the act, or the documentation, or the unseen response of the passer-by, or all of these?

LK: I don't regard the video as just a piece of documentation. My act of intervention can't become a performance with an audience as this would destroy the inconspic-uousness. Also the videos become narrative or sometimes even instructional.
The videos reveal the whole truth about my project, whereas the passer-by just sees somebody at work. When you watch the video you share the secret.

AM: So do you feel that your actions become understood as subversive through the existence and then presentation of a document? This creates two very specific audiences that witness your work, the art audience and the passer-by, one who understands it as subversive and the other who is subverted by it in some way.

'I installed locks into several phone boxes in London.'

LK: Yes, but don't forget, I also make other works where I subvert the people in the exhibition.

AM: What do you think about the potential for these gestures to be perceived as pranks?

LK: I feel quite comfortable being connected with jokes. A joke always has to be logical in itself, and an artwork as well. Both challenge so-called reality, but the difference is if someone is telling a joke in a social situation, we know it's a joke – this is quite important. In my case, when people are confronted with something that looks official, no one knows whether it's a joke or art.

AM: Have you ever felt as though you are helping to evolve the city through sidestepping the bureaucratic procedures typically necessary for change?

LK: I hope not.

Intercom, 2003
Video of intervention
Courtesy of the artist
and Corentin Hamel
Gallery, Paris

'I installed a loudspeaker of the Viennese public transport. Through a box with a microphone people can make their own announcements. The box is twenty meters away so the speaker stays anonymous.'

AM: What if your work became assimilated by society and eventually adapted and adopted to become a now integral part of how we understand the use of the phone box for example? In some ways you are giving the city something that it didn't know it needed.

LK: If this happened it would mean that there was no punchline, or that it was missed.

AM: Certain projects such as the phone box employ objects that are an iconic part of a particular city's heritage, but also objects the use of which is fading or has come to an end. Are you interested in evoking or awaking a community's nostalgia for their monuments or is it more an interest in the obsolescence of the situation itself?

LK: Changes to iconic sites are different because those sites are not functional. But I think the comparison with the past is quite interesting because it teaches us that in the past a different standard was seen as normal. It was standard that you could make a phone call in a separate room, protected against rain and noise, and also you had a degree of intimacy. Today everybody who does not want to be heard makes himself suspect.

AM: To plagiarize an interview question, I wondered if you had any projects that you felt were unrealizable based on legal or practical issues?

LK: All these interventions started with the impossibility of getting permission. A vague idea for a project starts with a situation. A situation is made out of possibilities and impossibilities. The first thing you mentioned to me concerning making a public intervention in London was that there is surveillance everywhere. So I had to find a place in the blind angle of the surveillance, at the same time public and not: the telephone box. The lock that secures the box corresponds now with the world of surveillance, but in fact the lock on the phone box creates a private space that protects you from surveillance. For me art is pretty much about turning disadvantages into advantages; it creates a process that tests the system from within.

AM: What would have been a failure?

LK: If there had already been locks in the phone boxes.

Aaron Moulton

Deimantas Narkevičius (b 1964)

In August 1991, fifty years of Soviet rule were dismantled in a central square of Vilnius, Lithuania's capital. A festive crowd gathered to witness the removal of the heroic statue of Lenin, which had been the city's most prominent example of monumental propaganda.

Once in the XX Century (2004), Deimantas Narkevičius's most recent film, returns us to the enthusiasm of those early post-Soviet years, when the future was the nation's only preoccupation. Recovering the TV footage that, more than a decade ago, recorded this event for Lithuanian television, Narkevičius brings it back to us with a sardonic twist. Sequence by sequence, the material has been skillfully edited so that we see, with astonishment and confusion, the statue being carefully *erected* in the midst of a celebrating multitude.

Silent witnesses of history, monuments become fixed incarnations of political regimes, carrying in their features the ideological and aesthetic values of their times. Rid of these landmarks, we lose the most eloquent references of a recent history; the ground of common understanding becomes as unstable as quicksand.

Once in the XX Century,
2004
Betacam SP video
printed on DVD, 8 min.
Courtesy of gb agency,
Jan Mot and the artist

Europa 54°54'–25°19',
1997, 16 mm film,
9 min.
Courtesy of gb agency,
Jan Mot and the artist

Narkevicius started using film during the early nineties. The camera offered him the possibility of exploring different narratives, allowing him to play with the course of time. In film he found a perfect medium for exploring both sound and visual language. *Europa 54°54'–25°19'* (1997) was filmed with a 16mm camera, recalling the documentary practice in 1970s Lithuania, when a crew was sent out during the early hours of the day to shoot footage or interviews that were later broadcast, almost unedited, on the evening news. In Narkevičius's film, the amateur camera follows an absurd journey from the artist's apartment block in Vilnius to the geographical centre of Europe, on the outskirts of the city. The film emphasises the relationship between geography and politics; the idea of the centre of Europe had no application in Soviet Lithuania, but now emerges to demonstrate Lithuania's place in the new ideological landscape of the European continent.

The slow rhythm of *Energy Lithuania* (2000) carries the viewer along in a gentle flow of images, documenting an old electric power plant built in the 1960s in Lithuania's countryside. Filmed with a 8mm camera, shots of the local dance school and swimming pool alternate with views of the interior and exterior of the plant. These images are inter-woven with interviews with people who worked there during the construction and early years of the plant, recalling the optimism of its beginnings.

The disjunctions between words and images in Narkevičius's films make manifest the impossibility of an objective documentary. He eschews the close-ups that are a common feature of contemporary documentaries, used to demonstrate the veracity of an interviewee's testimony. The central characters of Narkevicius's narratives are often absent from the screen, replaced by objects, drawings and other surrogates.

Energy Lithuania,
2000, Super 8 film
transferred onto DVD,
17 min.
Courtesy of gb agency,
Jan Mot and the artist

The two characters of *Kaimietis* (Countryman) (2002) remain off-screen while they offer their stories. Images of the streets of Vilnius are followed by close-ups of a Realist sculpture, portraying a Lithuanian national hero of the anti-Soviet armed resistance. The monument was commissioned from a young sculptor. While the camera gently lingers on the hard features of the hero, the sculptor reflects upon the meaning of the monument. The narrative breaks down and a young Lithuanian woman enters the film through a series of photographs that document her first day in a foreign country. The strong bond with her native country overrides the excitement of her journey; Lithuanian is the only language in which she can express her most intimate feelings. The music of Wagner's *Lohengrin* changes the rhythm of the narrative, infusing the scene with melancholy and evoking an overwhelming sense of loss as the camera lingers on a nondescript open space, a gap in the urban fabric.

Narkevičius's films exercise the intricate practice of memory and portray a contemporary society confronted with the painful processes of history. 'The ideological *orientation* that dominated for decades was – among other things – an attempt at creating a society above and beyond history. The new political situation re-inserted us into the rotating circuit of history, which inevitably requires a vision. (…) Things

Kaimietis
(Countryman), 2002
16 mm film transferred
onto video, 19 min.
Courtesy of gb agency,
Jan Mot and the artist

re-emerged from the past; phenomena that had been hidden under the surfaces of ideology. They led us into uncharted, unwanted, unpleasant territory, muddling our vision of the future.'[1]

Compared with his earlier films, *Once in the XX Century* is direct and unequivocal. It opposes the acts of erasure that commonly accompany 'regime change' and challenges the conventions enacted in these celebratory public moments. It acts to demonstrate the necessity of a visible historical heritage on which to build a shared future.

Carmen Juliá

1 Jonas Valatkevicius. E-mail conversation
Valatkevicius and Narkevicius, Autumn 2000
Biennale di Venezia 49 Lithuanian Pavillion
June 8 – November 4, 2001, p 25

Roman Ondák (b 1966)

The title of this exhibition derives, in amended and abbreviated form, from *Announcement* (2002), a work by Roman Ondák. The directive, 'As a sign of solidarity with recent world events, for the next minute do not interrupt the activity you are doing at this moment' takes the form of a radio broadcast. It was read in 2002 by a news presenter in the studios of International Radio Slovakia, recorded and since then heard in several European galleries and cities. Besides the work's ephemeral existence as a sound piece, it also exists in a printed edition on the back of Cologne Kunstverein's membership card for 2003. Just like the audio version, the printed form infiltrates the exhibition context and reminds people in unexpected moments of the reality that lies beyond the walls of the art institution.

In the Royal College of Art galleries, *Announcement* is transmitted so that the visitor hears the directive as if by accident while viewing the exhibition. Beginning with a temporal and spatial imprecision that renders the statement universally adaptable at all times, *'As a sign of solidarity with recent world events…'*, the call for non-action *'do not interrupt the activity you are doing at this moment'* is all the more disturbing since it is repetitive and present all over the space. The apparently innocent sentence, with its paradoxical request, is charged with all possible meanings attributed by each auditor.

This openness, as far as interpretation is concerned, is typical of Ondák's work. Sometimes slightly odd, his pieces are made to provoke wonder and suspicion, to prompt the spectator to spot the difference. In 2001, Ondák borrowed several old Skoda cars from Slovakia and parked them together behind the Secession in Vienna, a city from which they have nearly disappeared (*SK Parking*, 2001). The following year, for an exhibition at Spala Gallery in Prague, he invited a woman to teach her

Als ein Zeichen ihrer Solidarität mit den jüngsten Ereignissen in der Welt bitten wir Sie, die Tätigkeiten, die sie gerade ausüben, für die nächste Minute nicht zu unterbrechen

Announcement, 2003
Offset print on the back
of a membership card
Courtesy of Kölnischer
Kunstverein

baby how to walk in the space (*Teaching to Walk*, 2002). She would come daily for a little while and go away again. Rumours of something not quite right happening activate the audience who go looking for the artwork and wonder about its meaning. The opposite of spectacular, Ondák's actions seem so close to real situations that they sometimes don't get seen.

Tickets, Please (2002), presented in the same exhibition at Spala Gallery, was an equally discreet work that introduced another moment of confusion. Near the entrance, where one would usually find an elderly man sitting at a table selling catalogues and tickets to the exhibition, a young boy was sitting, asking for only half the entrance fee. Upstairs, exactly at the same location, on the same chair behind the same table, the old man one had expected downstairs, in fact the young boy's grandfather, requested the other half of the entrance fee. Another work which plays with the lapse of generations was produced by Ondák in *Tomorrows* (2002). The starting point of *Tomorrows* was to photograph local children in front of tourist monuments. The enlarged snapshots were then put up as posters on the town's walls – an eerie allusion to recent history with the omnipresence of party leaders' portraits dominating everyday life in former communist states.

For *Good Feelings in Good Times*, (2003–4), Ondák translated another characteristic of existence under communist times into a different context by hiring actors to

Good Feelings in Good Times, 2003–4
Artificially created queue
Performance at the
Frieze Art Fair, London
Tate Collection, London

Recording of Announcement in the Slovak Radio, Bratislava, 2002

form aimless queues inside or outside art institutions. Depending on the city it is performed in, *Good Feelings in Good Times* can be read in many ways. At Frieze Art Fair 2004, the queues evolved discreetly in and around the tent hosting the event, often unnoticed. Rarely talking to each other and waiting in front of a wall or outside the exhibition area before a locked fire exit, the actors looked so natural and patient that it seemed almost worth joining in. And indeed, sometimes, without a question, people would add themselves to this waiting group, expecting the time-consuming exercise to lead them to some desirable goal in the near future. They would sometimes stay up to ten minutes only to discover this action's lack of direction. That was one of the many reactions people could have in front of what, again, they often did not recognize as an artwork. In a London context and a busy art fair situation, *Good Feelings in Good Times* seemed to relate to the long waits suffered daily by London commuters, and to the trained-to-wait-patiently British society. These queues could also suggest, as the artist noted, that one should follow them 'to find a good orientation for 'better art' in this labyrinth of booths'.

Any interpretation is valid. Not knowing that *Good Feelings in Good Times* draws its inspiration from the artist's memories of queuing in communist Slovakia to get goods may not matter so much. What seems to matter is *how* Roman Ondák's staged situations – precisely often derived from personal or common lived experiences – are received, analysed, and experienced in the imagination of others, once transplanted into new environments, be they spatial, temporal, or social. Ultimately, the issue the artist raises is how these different time relations, newly formed meanings and often paradoxical perceptions develop and interconnect.

Anna Colin

Michael Rakowitz (b 1973)

Michael Rakowitz's practice uses social and urban infrastructure as a material, examining municipal loopholes and inconsistencies to reveal understated political issues or address repressed moments in history. *paraSITE* is a project initiated by the artist, providing homeless people with inflatable shelters that attach to building ventilation systems.

AM: *paraSITE* is a collaborative project in which the homeless users of the structures are deeply involved. Can you describe this process?

MR: I produce each shelter to the custom specifications of each homeless inhabitant, to directly influence this device with the actual experience of someone who lives on the streets of the city. In Boston, when I presented the idea to a group of homeless men, they discouraged the use of the standard black trash bags that I employed as a material for my first prototype, for the purpose of establishing some sense of privacy. Their critique was that they did not have privacy issues, but rather security issues: they wanted to see potential attackers and they wanted to be seen. Also, visibility established some kind of equality and interrupted their 'normal' invisibility in the public realm. In this way, the project communicates on the level of sign or symbol back to a pedestrian public about some of the specific topographies of this invisible or marginalized citizenry and, in many cases, the unacceptable circumstances of their daily life.

AM: How did *paraSITE* come to be exhibited in museums and galleries?

MR: Documentation of the work first appeared in architecture books and then in the New York Times 'Metro' section in late December 1999. This was appropriate and very valuable in terms of a discourse about the work, avoiding immediate attachment to artistic practice. It was through this direct urban and human context that the project became known. Documentation of *paraSITE* has been exhibited in many venues over the past five years, concurrent with its primary existence as an urban intervention on the streets.

AM: Since the project has entered the gallery, how has the art setting changed the nature of the project or the way it has been mediated to (or interpreted by) a general public who might otherwise have encountered it on the streets?

MR: Your questions concerning the affect of the structure's exhibition in the gallery context resonate with me, because this was a struggle for me to consider and eventually allow. When I had first shown the work at White Columns, I was adamant in not presenting a prototype. For me, the project belonged on the streets, directly interfacing with the life of its intended user, not in some exhibition institution seemingly disconnected from the project's intended context. But something interesting happened around the winter of 2001: one of the homeless men named Bill Stone called to tell me that he was no longer homeless, that he had beaten his alcohol problem, and that he had found employment. He no longer needed the shelter and had his municipal support group send it back. For a long while curators had inquired about having some physical representation of the actual structures in the exhibition space, which I had flat out rejected: I refused to use my energy in the production of a prototype, specifically for exhibition. But when I received Bill's shelter back in the mail, I realized that the structures themselves could broadcast the narrative, if not something of the personality of the individual who had used them, in a very different way than photographs.

AM: And that's how one of the actual units became an exhibit?

MR: Yes. One unit was shown at the National Design Triennial at the Cooper-Hewitt in 2003. In this highly visible context, an exhibition presenting progress and success in the field of design, I felt as though the project could argue for a certain type of strategy for the marginalized. As an object among objects, it lobbied for a design practice or, at the very least, a new form of radical design research in which designers might turn their attention toward the creation of devices or equipment

paraSITE,
1998–ongoing
Photograph courtesy
of the artist

for those who are most in need, and away from the tendency to create (in Victor Papanek's terms) the 'idiot gadget', the luxury device, the 14K gold-plated Nokia phone. When I first installed the piece, the unit was obviously quite tarnished from its function which was on the street and I explicitly told the preparators not to clean it up as its origins were important in disclosing its history.

AM: Is this one of the strategies you employ to save your structures from being aestheticized as design or as a sculptural objects?

MR: Yes. Whenever a prototype is exhibited, it is required that the exhibition institution also presents, through photos or video, documentation of the shelter's use on the street and the description or story that accompanies the individual and the *paraSITE*. I also make a request that the shelter be attached to the building's exterior or interior ventilation system, to at least conceptually or psychologically connect the work to its critical moment.

AM: What would you say are the positive effects of exhibiting the project in art institutions?

MR: The gallery context has expanded the project's realm of dissemination and discourse. While the project is public, the exchange and dialogue that occurs between each homeless individual and myself as a part of the process is a critical moment in the work that is not immediately visible or accessible to the pedestrian encountering the shelters on the street. The exhibition space has afforded the project an opportunity to broadcast these narrative transactions in the form of writings, film and photographic documentation, as well as open the project up to citizens who may not encounter the work in the city.

paraSITE,
1998–ongoing
Photograph courtesy
of the artist

paraSITE,
1998–ongoing
Photograph courtesy
of the artist

AM: *paraSITE* has obvious links to the mobile homeless shelters made by your former professor Krzysztof Wodiczko in the eighties. How does your work in this area compare to or differ from Wodiczko's?

MR: I am an admirer of his work and his methodologies of addressing problems through the proposition of further problems. I see him as a pioneer of work in this area. However we diverge in where we are coming from. My own interests in nomadism extend from my mother's family's history as Jews who were exiled from Iraq in 1946. This interest led to my participation in an MIT-sponsored architectural residency in Jordan in 1997. While there, I had focused on the tents and equipment of the Bedouin. As nomadic desert tribes, their shelters take into account the way that the wind moves through the desert via a sort of aerodynamics. It was out of this practical approach that I was able to translate that method to another type of nomadism.

Back in Boston, I was enrolled in a course, entitled Nomadic Design, of which Krzysztof was one of the professors. The limitations of the model-making/pin-up drawing phase that is characteristic of architecture studio classes led me to move into the environment and engage the actual people who would potentially use these devices to get an idea of how to make this work.

What differentiates the two projects, I think, is that while Wodiczko's *Homeless*

(P)LOT,
2003–ongoing
Photograph courtesy of
the Museum Moderner
Kunst Stiftung Ludwig
Wien (Vienna)

Vehicle is somewhat autonomous and self-sufficient, I was interested in the poetry that existed in the critical moment of *paraSITE*, as an inflatable connected to a building, as an organism attached to a host. It becomes an inversion of the architecture, of the inside out into the outside, and for me the project came alive at that point. As soon as *paraSITE* becomes autonomous, as soon as it is removed from the host edifice, it becomes non-functional and independent, and perhaps literally loses its attachment to the situation. Maintaining the DIY structure, this clear notion of portraiture, and the poetry, have been important to me from the beginning. Enlisting each person as an entity and addressing these people as citizens has been the goal. I understand Wodiczko's homeless vehicle as existing as both a utility and protest device that is potent, now and especially during the era of its creation, the late 1980s in New York City. This period witnessed some of the most insidious municipal policies concerning the homeless crisis and inspired unprecedented resistance and in some cases solidarity (for example, the Tompkins Square Park demonstrations). *Homeless Vehicle* was effective as a design object that, in Wodiczko's terms, scandalises functionalism, communicating empowerment among the city's vanquished through the once harmless vocabulary and utility of the shopping cart. It is the product of an intense and careful design process. In *paraSITE*, I locate a hybrid situation of tailor-making based on individual needs, simultaneously relinquishing my control as a designer.

AM: *paraSITE* has already moved from Boston to Baltimore and New York. Would you consider taking the project out of the States to, say, London?

MR: *paraSITE* is a device for protest and also effective survival, but it is also about an exchange between the person making it and the person using it. There is a heavy degree of site-specificity to *paraSITE* and that's what makes it interesting. It might not be meant to adapt, but at least it can start the discussion about where one can take advantage of municipal availability within systems and somehow circumvent them. It reveals other methodologies for how to get around a challenge, but is also a perfect device for proposing other projects.

AM: Has *paraSITE* manifested itself differently, accommodating to the limitations of a situation or to address different issues altogether?

MR: A new project that I have introduced first in Vienna and more recently in Milan and Trento, Italy is *(P)LOT*. *(P)LOT* questions the occupation and dedication of public space and encourages reconsiderations of 'legitimate' participation in city life. Contrary to the common procedure of using municipal parking spaces as storage surfaces for vehicles, *(P)LOT* proposes the rental of these parcels of land for alternative purposes. The acquisition of municipal permits and simple payment of parking meters could enable citizens to, for example, establish temporary encampments or use the leased ground for different kinds of activities. A first initiative for this re-dedication is realized through the conversion of ordinary car covers into portable tents, available for loan at MUMOK (the Museum of Modern Art in Vienna) and other art institutions. Visitors to the museum and interested citizens who wish to participate in the development of this proposed culture will have the choice to use one of five covers ranging from a common sedan to a luxurious Porsche or motorcycle, thereby enabling a broadcast of desire within the marginalized space of need. Future incarnations of this project will include ad-hoc gardens and public barbecues in these spaces, as well as the construction of scaled down football goals to be placed at either end of an entire city block worth of spaces where a group of children will play a football game within these new margins.

Aaron Moulton

Reader
Eilidh MacAskill (b 1980)
Robert Walton (b 1980)
Lalage Harries (b 1977)
James Leadbitter (b 1980)

Lalage Harries, Eilidh MacAskill and Robert Walton form the core of collaborative performance group Reader. In their site-specific and durational events, they address 'the big subjects of life, liberty and lemmings'. They profess to delight in 'simultaneously charming and terrorising the public with all the aplomb found in society, government and the media'.

Many of Reader's performances explore the issues of relationships and inter-personal communication. *Strangers and Intimacy* (2004) is a collaboration with four artists from Australia. In preparation for a residency in Melbourne, the members of Reader engaged in writing letters to local artists. The weekly correspondence aimed to help the strangers get to know each other before they met in the flesh and started working together. In an age of proliferating email and cyber cultures, the antiquated gesture of becoming pen-pals appears romantic and reminiscent of childhood times. Moreover, this interaction played with notions of self-portrayal and perception, for what is a pen-pal if not someone about whom we imagine more than we actually know, about whom we must place faith in what the other tells us?

An event that promised to be nothing less than *A meeting to decide upon the nature of a new planet and its contents* (July 2003) was a conference of seven hours, during which papers from Reader's 'esteemed colleagues' were heard on subjects such as *Scorpions and Cake*, *Waking Up and Excess* and *Eating and Mist*. From the outset the symposium was designed to highlight its own over-ambition and unfeasibility. For every topic that was touched on, a thousand others were passed over. The topics discussed at the performance were intended to act simply as a narrative to engage with temporarily, a fictitious encyclopaedia that could only ever be completed in the imagination of each individual viewer.

The performance *Special Relationship* (November 2002), which involved the active involvement of the audience, subjected the participant to feelings of unease and discomfort resulting from authoritative behaviour. Each participant had to pick a card that provided one of four different options and to follow the instructions written on that card. Each participant was made to sign a disclaimer and had thumbprints taken. From there, he or she was led by a silent guide into a tent

where the participants were put through different forms of interrogation. He was never verbally or physically forced, though, only whispered at and subtly coerced.

During the performance, the participants were simultaneously engaged in different activities, so that each person could only see one part of the whole event. Although they remained aware that they were involved in a fictitious set-up, most felt that to pull out or to stop the performance would have been more unbearably embarrassing than to carry on with it.

For *Do Not Interrupt Your Activities* Reader will present a series of twenty papers, semi-improvised lectures on the subject of human relationships, each twenty minutes long. The seven-hour performance, *Can't you hear me? It's dark in here. Where have you gone anyway?: Weathering the storms of human relations*, aims to investigate and settle any possible difficulty arising from mistakes or bad behaviour in all forms of human interaction, thus working towards a trouble-free future for all. Reader will go on to elucidate the subjects of human/animal, human/object and human/landscape relationships. Throughout the entire performance, the relations between the members of Reader will serve as a showcase example of 'good interaction'. Not only will the audience have the chance to listen to speeches elaborating on how to avoid the common problems in human relationships, we shall also be able to witness the practical application of Reader's advice.

Strangers and Intimacy, 2004–5
Westspace Gallery, Melbourne, Australia
Performance collaboration made during a residency with CCA, Glasgow
Photograph courtesy of Reader

During the entire performance, members of the audience are at liberty to come and go as they please, but while in the performance space, they may be asked to participate, to answer questions or to voice an opinion on whatever topic is currently being discussed. Forced to participate actively in this mock symposium, the audience has to suspend disbelief in the very nature of the conversation and collaborate in the pretence. The participants are in a position of power, able to change and influence the conversation, but they are only thus privileged because they have been put there by a member of Reader. Participants are in fact under the performers' control, forced to adhere to their arbitrary decisions.

Rose Lejeune

'Can't you hear me? It's dark in here. Where have you gone anyway?'
Weathering the storms of human relations: A symposium, 2005
Durational Performance Event Commissioned for *Do Not Interrupt Your Activities*

Giorgio Sadotti (b 20th century)

Giorgio Sadotti sits on the fence. In his work he crosses the boundaries between the roles of curator, artist and gallery. A vigilant and critical observer of the commercial art scene, Sadotti undermines the gallery system and its inherent rules and social structures.

In his most radical work to date, Giorgio Sadotti surrendered a slice of his own life. For his project *Be Me* (1996), he invited thirty artist friends to do exactly that, to be him. Taking on different aspects of his persona, over the course of one whole month Sadotti's friends were allowed to do as they pleased. Whatever they did during that time, Sadotti was accountable for. One alter Giorgio made a rubber cast of his nose and wore it over hers. One went out for dinner with Sadotti's gallerist, another 'Giorgio' went to Manchester and made a film about the artist's parents. Another participant had decided that if she was to be Sadotti, then he should be her. She organised a public artist/curator talk during which she and Sadotti performed reversed roles, which resulted in Sadotti asking questions about his own work. One pseudo-Giorgio even slept with the artist's girlfriend and brought the bed sheets to the gallery as a record of the event. During the entire project, videos, audiotapes and photographs were made, which were exhibited in the gallery to cumulatively build up to the exhibition. By relinquishing his authority as the sole person able to execute his work, Sadotti constructed a self-portrait moulded by thirty different readings of his persona.

Be Me, 1996
Live event at
Maureen Paley/Interim
Art, London
Photograph courtesy
of the artist

Dinner (1996) at Cubitt Gallery London was both dinner event and exhibition. Actually, it was an exhibition curated by Sadotti that took the form of a dinner. Sadotti had asked seven artists to each take care of, design and prepare a specific facet of the meal, from the crockery to the social agenda. The artists received detailed instructions for the tasks that were allocated to them which left little room for artistic freedom or manoeuvre: Gavin Turk was asked to create the napkins, Angela Bulloch to make a soundtrack, and Liam Gillick to design the dinner plates. Patricia Bickers wrote an after-dinner speech, and Rachel Evans conceived the menu. For the event, Sadotti had invited curators, critics and collectors, but not the participating artists, and he did not attend either. He had reduced the artists to service providers – an acid comment on the relationship and the power balance within the gallery system. After the dinner, the table and all detritus remained in the gallery as a record of the event.

Many of Sadotti's works reference the happenings and actions of the Fluxus generation. While the residue table of *Dinner* loosely evokes Spoerri's 'tableaux-pièges', *Went To America, Didn't Say a Word* (1999) recalls Beuys's famous expedition to the United States. Sadotti travelled to New York for one day without uttering a single word. Walking around the city he recorded all voices approaching him, all surrounding noises, which now form his sound-piece of the same title. Sadotti's silence is an act of refusal, a refusal to engage and to participate in a particular society, a mute protest against the Americanisation of language and culture. *Violin Siren* (2004) translates one particular sound of the city into the realms of music and art, calling to mind the musical trespassing of Satie or Cage. *Violin Siren* is performed by four violin players who, in conjunction with Sadotti, have

Violin Siren, 2004
Live event at P.S.1
Contemporary Art
Center, New York
Photograph courtesy
of the artist

individually created a score that mimics the sound of an emergency services siren. While playing their instruments the performers pace through the exhibition space, disrupting all other sound and conversation. Sadotti gives sound, which exists only in an ephemeral, abstract form, a face and a sculptural existence.

Sadotti occupies an artistic position that deliberately and very consciously refuses to fit into any category, allowing him to conceive projects that try to cancel each other out and that refuse to sit comfortably within the confines of the art gallery. Sadotti borrowed his motto from Groucho Marx: 'I wouldn't want to belong to any club that would have me as a member', and so he continues to sit on the fence. It is usually considered an uncomfortable place to be, but for now Sadotti is happy with the view from up there.

Sarah McCrory

Yara El-Sherbini (b 1978)

Yara El-Sherbini's practice engages with current world political situations, focusing on areas of personal interest. She refers to herself as British, Egyptian, Trinidadian and Muslim, and the complex identity politics born of this background are a source of continual exploration in her work, especially with reference to the contemporary global issues that connect to her sense of identity. Sherbini adopts a fluid approach to medium, working with intervention, installation, internet-based digital media, text, sculpture, and performance.

Like many artists, Sherbini finds some form of private catharsis in her work. The frenetic pace at which she works, rarely pausing for answers before moving on to the next pressing project, is testament to the intensity of her feelings, the urgency of her need to articulate her frustrations.

Sherbini's *UN Survival Kit* (2002) was an accurate parody of the UN survival kits that are sent to troubled areas in times of disaster. Sherbini sent this revised kit to Kofi Annan and other members of the Security Council while one copy was kept for gallery display. With acid humour, Sherbini pointed to the sheer inefficacy of some of the UN kits' contents, such as the toilet rolls sent to Mozambique after

A Demonstration, 2005, Performance Commissioned for *Do Not Interrupt Your Activities* Photograph courtesy of the artist

the floods which had destroyed all drainage systems. In response, Sherbini's kit contained *Item No. 6 – Toilet 'Role' : United 'States'*. Upon this *Toilet Role* was printed an American flag, in which the stars representing states were replaced with stars of David. This intervention manifested her outrage at the apparent full and total support of America toward the massacres of Palestinians perpetrated by Israelis, and their continued illegal occupation of Palestinian lands. *Item no. 5 – Food Ration, Jelly Kit* offered the recipient a chance to make jelly in a UN mould. Such dark humour is the vehicle for her deeply critical stance. The motivation for the work was in part Sherbini's fear that the UN was becoming no more than a conscience-salving set of abstract ideals, as opposed to an effective defender of democracy and humanitarian values.

In *A Demonstration*, the workshop-performance commissioned for this exhibition, Sherbini turns a familiar term into an absurd visual and verbal pun, and a devastating act of war becomes an item you can make and take home. The participant may choose between Middle Eastern prayer mat, English floral or bland institutional carpet samples and different sized balls to make their unique bomb. Crafting the bomb is a strenuous, time-consuming task for the visitor. Working around a table together, the artist and audience are given an informal forum for discussion. There is a refreshing ingenuity in the appropriation of the educative workshop format which forms the crux of the work.

Sherbini's work plays with language, exploring the shared understanding of cultural, social and political references that make a joke funny. Her sharp wit and her stated intention not to try and change the world, but rather to ask questions on a personal level, absolve her of any accusations of didacticism. She harbours no illusions that her work will necessarily force the viewer to reassess their perceptions of the world but is committed to making us look at what we think in a new way.

Rebecca May Marston

Christian Sievers (b 1974)

In his lecture performances Christian Sievers has developed a peculiar format involving a vast collection of images presented as a slide show alongside a scripted text. His scripts often collage together contradictory impressions and opinions that he has gathered through questionnaires.

Sievers's presence on stage evokes a sense of vulnerability, an uncomfortable moment of *mise à nu*. Like a test one has to pass in front of an audience, Sievers's difficult presentation often concludes with a personal process of understanding and resolving the issue raised in his performance. The ostensibly severe lecture performances, however, are lightened by humour and parody.

What follows are excerpts from a conversation which took place in south London in February 2005.

AC: What made you choose the particular format of your performances?

CS: I once had a strange encounter when I was still at college. I showed someone around who was interested in studying there. She appeared a bit confused, said thanks and left. A few weeks later I received a VHS tape from her. It said on it that

On Tough Guys and Soft Guys, 2003
Lecture Performance

you could play it only once and then it would self-destruct. I gathered some friends to watch it with me. It was very short and very weird. I still don't know what it was. I've always found that extremely interesting: What do you see if you know you won't get another look?

AC: By adopting the slide lecture format, you engage the viewer in an experience similar to the one you have just described, in so far as the projection of images is a consecutive act where each image is shown once in a linear progression. As a result, one is likely to concentrate harder. What matters to you in the act of showing your pictures to others and what does that process help you realise?

CS: I've always liked showing slides of my work. In college you have to do it all the time. Some people hate it. It always gave me the opportunity to look at the images in a fresh way, and by talking about it with others, to change their meaning. When I got my first digital camera, I took thousands and thousands of photos. All kinds, from snapshots of family and friends, to streets and landmarks. Then, as I was going through these pictures, I started to identify certain recurring themes and sculptural issues. When I started working on *Tough Guys and Soft* Guys, I had been thinking about hard and soft sculpture for a while. I suppose the title came from a TV review of a programme where a British man went to live with an Ethiopian family and go hungry for a month. It said he was a soft man who does a tough thing. After editing the images down from an initial trawl of several hundred, they ended up being photos of my friends. Who all turned out to be softies. The lectures are a methodical way to identify those unresolved questions, filtered down from this large archive of images. I can draw in other, disparate material, and expand my understanding of the problem. I always need material to fill some missing link so I'm constantly on the lookout. It all feeds into the next lecture. Everything is connected to everything else. I enjoy that.

AC: On what subject did you base your first performances?

CS: Originally, the lecture series were supposed to be some kind of personal news update. They were called *The Christian Sievers News of the World* and took place monthly. It went on for two or three months, but soon became impossible to sustain. Also, there wasn't that much happening.

AC: To your life?

CS: To my life and also to the world. It was the beginning of 2003 and the war in Iraq was about to start. Everybody was angry, and all you could do was to watch. When I say the exercise went on for only a few months it is because I never considered the third lecture finished. It was called *On Look But Don't Touch*.

It was a pretty tough piece about powerlessness, even more so since the text was very personal. But at least I managed to keep my eyes open. The images were of barriers, fences and other obstructing devices in the street; reflective and fogged-up windows.

When asked to propose a work for *Do Not Interrupt Your Activities* I thought I would come back to this lecture and finish it. I have sent out a questionnaire to friends and acquaintances and asked among other questions: 'What do you prefer, darkness or light?' and 'Where would you rather be right now?' Somebody answered: 'I like sex in the dark'. This funny quote summed up quite well the issue of whether you prefer to see or not to see. Another person said: 'It's easier to orientate and tell colours apart, without light I could not work, shower, cook, drive a car, could not tell who is in front of me or which is the way home.'

AC: Are there any disciplines located outside the arts that inform your practice?

CS: The Wunderkammer approach interests me. This is the German term for cabinet of curiosity. It is a collection of everything there is in the world gathered in one room. It leads to asking questions about the world and how these objects relate to each other. My lectures work similarly. An image of the world in 30 photos is a bit like a baroque Wunderkammer. It also makes me think of German art historian

Aby Warburg and *Image-Atlas MNEMOSYNE*, the great atlas of the visual world he developed in the 1920s.

AC: How these objects relate to each other is not only up to the person who has installed them, but also relies on the narrative or interpretation supplied by the viewer. This is also true of your performances that, at first glance, look very formal and prepared, but are at the same time cryptic and very open to various interpretations.

CS: Yes, and regularly people come to me at the end to tell me about the connections they have made, often ideas I had never thought of during the research process.

Anna Colin

Song Dong (b 1966)

Since 1995, Song Dong has been keeping a diary, written in water on stone. The events and feelings recorded disappear and are written over, again and again. Its secrets evaporate, leaving only the memory of the action. This ongoing, intensely intimate performance, *Writing Diary with Water* (1995–present) is documented in only four close-up photographs of wet characters on the stone. The idea exists instead in time and imagination. In this meditative act, Song Dong makes time to reflect on the experience of living. He writes down that which he cannot speak, in an endless therapeutic ritual.

Writing a diary can be dangerous, you cannot write down something you would not want someone else to read one day. Song Dong's impalpable journal, however, is secure, what he has written can never be retrieved. He tells how he adamantly refused when a collector offered a high sum to try and persuade him to sell the diary stone – it has become part of his body. It is a totemic object, absorbing neurosis and worry. As the artist knows he can confide anything in it, he feels freer, less anxious. He says that he writes to release emotions, and watch the words disperse and drift away, without suffering consequences. He invites visitors to similarly unburden themselves in his installation *You Can Write Anything With*

Writing Diary with Water, 1995–present
Colour photograph
Courtesy of the artist

Water (2004). It is the experiential, pleasurable, bodily aspect of writing, which is of primary significance to Song Dong, not its function as a means of communicating information.

Song Dong finds oblique ways to express political dissent in the face of radical social change. He discovers new meanings in everyday activities such as breathing and writing. Conceptually and formally his works are beautifully integrated. His works leave no permanent trace beyond a couple of photographs and the memory. His poetic, futile gestures can offer us profound personal and political insight.

Breathing (1996) was a performance which took place at two locations in Beijing, Tiananmen Square, and Houhai Lake, a pond in the old part of the city. The artist lay face-down at these two places and breathed onto the ground steadily for 40 minutes, attempting to leave a frozen trace of his breath. *Breathing* is documented in two large photographs and a recording of the artist's breathing.

The first image shows Song Dong, sharply foregrounded, alone on the cement at night, an illuminated Tiananmen in the background. It is New Year's Eve 1996 and the temperature is -9°C. *Breathing* can be read as a tribute to the pro-democracy June Fourth Movement, whose violent suppression in Tiananmen Square has left an ugly scar on China's national psyche and international reputation. Song Dong's forty minutes of exertion, in this passionate, solitary act of peaceful protest, left a frozen puddle on the ground, a dark trace. It was gone the next morning, like the bloodstains of the protestors. He tries to infuse life into the square, imploring its freezing, unforgiving surface to accept the gift of his warm breath. His futile act underscores the difficulties inherent in an individual's attempt to engender change.

In *Breathing* Song Dong lies prone on the inanimate ground, vulnerable, as if in surrender. Breathing is the basic indication that you are alive. Breathing is an involuntary action; you do not have to think about it. Song Dong makes it into a concentrated act of will. The small pool of ice he leaves may be temporary but has powerful meaning. On Houhai Lake, in an everyday neighbourhood, the pond's frozen surface merely absorbed his breath organically, as water fused with ice, and the artist appears like Narcissus, transfixed by his own reflection.

Stamping the Water (1996) consists of 36 photographs which document Song Dong's performance in the Lhasa River, Tibet. He stamped the sacred water for an hour with a large traditional seal engraved with the Chinese character for 'water'. Like King Cnut sitting in the waves, Song Dong takes on the exhausting, Sisyphean task of stamping man's ownership on this ever-moving mass. The seal, however, leaves no trace and the power of the symbol is neutered.

This heroic but futile gesture also comments on the absurdity of current efforts to assert ownership of a river. Lhasa is on the contested border of China and Tibet and both countries claim its water.

Fill the Sea (1997) is a series of 158 photographs documenting each step of a performance carried out on the shore at Shen Zhen between the Chinese mainland and Hong Kong. Song Dong was inspired by the myth of a girl who drowned crossing the sea here and was transformed into a bird. In her new incarnation, she devoted her life to trying to fill up the sea with small stones. Song Dong threw 158 stones, one by one, into the sea at this spot. On each stone, using water, he had written one of the years of the British occupation of Hong Kong. He began with 1840, the year of the Opium War, and ended with 1997 when Hong Kong was returned to China. It was a futile attempt to reverse the flow of history. It was a poetic and precise political act of commemoration.

More recently, Song Dong has turned his attention to rapid urban development in China, where bland skyscrapers appear overnight and all that is solid melts into air. He observes the destruction of traditional buildings and the rash transformation of the city, collecting relics from bulldozed houses. He prises the shiny veneer off the city to reveal the psychic scars beneath and mourn ways of life that have changed irrevocably.

He creates visual parallels between the destruction of buildings and the decon-struction of their representational images. In several works he indulges in fantasies

You Can Write Anything With Water, 2004
Chinese Arts Centre,
Manchester
Photograph:
Ali MacGilp

of destroying China's cityscapes while punning on the surface of the film screen. In *Crumpling Shanghai* (2000) the city is projected onto a sheet of rice paper which fills the screen, and the artist's hand, like a giant's, crushes China's fastest-changing, most frenetic city. In *Broken Mirror* (1999) and *Burning Mirror* (2001) an urban scene of Beijing is reflected in a mirror, which is quickly shattered or slowly burned away to reveal the view through the looking glass. In *Floating* (2004) mundane pans of new shopping areas and building sites in Beijing are projected onto a bucket of water and Song Dong dips his hand into the surface, writing numbers, marking time, distorting the image. He makes us aware of the illusion of China's booming economy, the disconnection between public spectacle and personal experience. He wonders how to find a place within this brave new world.

Ali MacGilp

Kate Stannard (b 1981)

Missing things – a lack of substance – an empty package.
Missing things – an inability to find the Thing.
Hurriedly flooding through the streets of Glasgow each morning, I observe a sea of
drawn white faces: lifeless, colourless, bloodless. I imagine that if these bodies cut
themselves shaving nothing would leak out but stagnant air.
It does not sicken me as much as scare me, as I recognise one of those lined,
hollow, pale faces to be my own reflection.
Eleven months ago an angry drunken Swiss woman said to me 'K...you uphold
everything European woman see British women as being. You are without
substance. In these times of war where is your blood?'
Whiteness. White faces, white eyes, white fingers.
White sliced bread, white ice cream, white sugar, white flour.
Refined, bleached, artificial, processed, produced, true colour and substance
removed. Industrialised and economically efficient.
Socially produced and materialistically packaged.
Pale and without substance. This loaf of bread, this body.[1]

Kate Stannard's wide-ranging practice embraces performance, theatre and visual
art. In her work she focuses on her body and the way it communicates and
functions within society. She confronts those things that fascinate and disgust her.
She describes her panic and distress at the ocean of ashen, lifeless faces
surrounding her every morning. She imagines these people, amongst whom she
includes herself, with only stagnant air coursing through their veins; bloodless
and passionless. The first part of *Missing Things* is a healing ritual that attempts
to retrieve this missing colour. Stannard first performed *Missing Things* at the
National Review of Live Art in 2004, after being selected as one of the most
promising young artists of the 2003 festival.

Missing Things 2,
September 2004
Performed at The
Merchant City Festival,
Glasgow, with support
from the National
Review of Live Art
and New Moves
International

1 Kate Stannard in
New Territories
brochure (New Moves
International, 2004,
p 41)

Missing Things 1,
February 2004
A 'One Year On'
commission for the
National Review of Life
Art, 2004 performed at
The Arches, Glasgow,
with support from CCA

During the seven-hour performance, Stannard works with loaves of sliced white bread and bright red thread. She crumbles, stitches and models slices of bread into doughy sculptural forms, saturating the objects with her physical intensity using her hair and saliva in this creative process. Stannard positions the bread forms in seven stark shafts of light that fall across the floor. She then places white carnations in vases of red liquid. The flowers drink this blood-like fluid and their pure, anaemic colour becomes stained as they gain a life-force. Stannard's symbolic activities reflect the artificial and soulless nature of urban living. Stannard uses this white bread, with its doughy flesh, as a surrogate for her body and the bodies around her. Pallid skin, processed bread, refined sugar, bleached flour, all 'pale and without substance' are the consequences of industrialised efficiency.

Every performance of *Missing Things* changes the work. There is an incremental addition of both perceptible and imperceptible changes. *Missing Things* has developed a second part, in which Stannard painstakingly undoes all of the actions in Part 1 over a further seven-hour period. After the apparent catharsis of Part 1, she now draws the colour out of the flowers and presses the bread flat again. This reverse process suggests, perhaps, that the current state of society is incurable. Stannard's personal beliefs have evolved as she has developed the work since it was first performed. From a contradictory tangle of perceptions she has distilled the indisputable fact that 'it's all just birth, death and sex.'

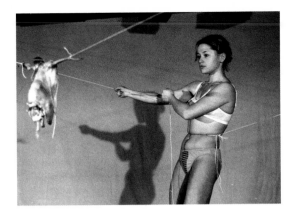

Lifedrawing,
March 2002
Performed at
Tramway, Glasgow
Photograph:
Fiona Cole

The artist's struggle in *Missing Things* echoes an earlier performance, *Lifedrawing* (2001/3), in which Stannard makes visible the interior forms of her body, on its surface. Onstage she traces the lines of the muscles, bones and creases of her face, hands and body on her skin with thick black marks. Stannard explores the limits of her physicality, contrasting it with that of a fresh chicken carcass, which acts as a bodily substitute. She binds herself to the chicken, plays with it like a puppet and dances with it before, finally, dissecting it.

Stannard's most recent investigations into her body are the ongoing collaborations between herself and the artist Sarah Potter as *The Dirty Girls*. Together, they explore the idea of 'emotional dirt': emotional baggage and the guilt, shame and fear that results from our social conditioning. They ask how as young, educated, white, Western women living today, they can deal with this dirt. *The Dirty Girls* pepper their process of exploration with performances, installations and actions. In one performance, they adopt the alter egos of the smutty girls they love to hate, the girls who do the things they could never do. In another they are angel-faced, banana-eating, pink-clad nymphs who invite you to peek at their acridly-perfumed installations in the downstairs toilet of Glasgow's Tramway. Stannard and Potter are more interested in the process of making art, than in packaging a finished product. They allow changing personal circumstances to lead the development of their work over time.

Rebecca May Marston

Talkaoke (Michael Weinkove) (b 1974)

Michael Weinkove's *Talkaoke* has become a regular feature at bars, galleries and events in London since 1997. This travelling talk show has evolved from an informal forum to an all-in-one 'porta-table', complete with confident host.

SM: How did the first Talkaoke come about?

MW: Some people I went to college with were organising a live art nightclub called the Hydra Club at the Vibe Bar in Brick Lane. They wanted me to repeat a performance I did in 1994 and 1995 at the Cardiff Art in Time Festival. It was called *It's Your Shout!* and was like a TV forum but with no agenda. At the time I was fascinated with the show Kilroy, because I found Kilroy and the show really objectionable, but still found it really compelling. If I had to go in early to college I used to tape it. The thing that upset me the most about the show was that it was totally choreographed. Kilroy knew what everybody was going to say and he just moved from person to person and gave them the mike to blurt out their prearranged statement without really listening and taking part in any constructive debate. But people seemed to be so energised by taking the mike and saying their thing nevertheless.

The show *It's Your Shout!* seemed like a good way of tying up some of the threads of my practice. At the time I was concerned with the baffling, infinite 'unknow-ableness' of human knowledge, how every idea was connected, with politics, with systems that have non-determined outcomes, but mostly with the problem of contemporary alienation, particularly apparent in our city. Also there was something really attractive and scary about performing when you had no idea of what you were supposed to be doing.

I wasn't really pleased with the outcome of *It's Your Shout!* People didn't take it seriously and express their opinions earnestly. What did I expect? They were suspicious of me. Nevertheless people went away with that confused, headfuck feeling they've come to expect from live art. So Gini Simpson from Hydra asked me to put on this show for their night at the Vibe Bar. There was no budget for the show, and the previous *It's Your Shout!* took days of organisation and the combined AV resources of St Martins and Cardiff. So I tried to think of how I could scale it down. Instead of a big forum I would have a round table, etc. etc. I was very pleased with the outcome. People talked more earnestly in this more intimate setting, but still got a thrill from ranting on the microphone. The conversation was interesting, thoughtprovoking. It got people who didn't know each other talking. It was only supposed to be a one-off but they asked me to come back again and again until it became a regular feature. Eventually I became a regular at another club, Duckie, and the flying saucer of chat took off.

SM: During a performance, how do you establish a relationship with your audience/participants?

MW: The most important thing when starting off a *Talkaoke* is to be yourself. Don't be scared of who you are. In my case and anybody else who wants to host *Talkaoke* we have a genuine desire to talk to people to find out what they think, be creative together to make something new, albeit something as small as a conversation. There are questions of ambiences and moods too.

Generally when I do a *Talkaoke* there are a few people around and they either know about *Talkoake* or they're curious about the sci-fi looking table. All I need is for a couple of people to sit down to get the show going. Sometimes I just start talking on my own about anything and encouraging people to come and sit down.

The first *Talkaokes* were not always successful. Sometimes I was left isolated in the middle there. I didn't have the confidence in the early days to just keep going. The Live Art crowd loved this. They loved the risk, the pain, the critique of society.

Talkaoke,
1997–present
Photograph courtesy
of the artist

Are we all shits?', that kind of thing. I thought it was rubbish. I felt I failed. So I 'started to develop techniques to get people talking. The first way I did this was to make sure that my friends were there at the start of the show. We called this stooging' although the stooges didn't have anything specific to say. They just talked 'about what they wanted to talk about. Nor did they deny they knew me. I used stooges up until 2002, but now I am more confident and have more subtle ways of getting people involved.

SM: You've talked about isolation and the lack of conversation you've noticed between strangers, can you talk more about this?

MW: 'Imagine 7 million people all wanting to live together'. That's what Crocodile Dundee said or something like that. One of the most common themes in contemporary culture is alienation and isolation from each other. Go and see *Lost In Translation*. I'm not going to go into my beliefs on the reasons for this. Suffice to say there's a lot of it about. Every tube journey is an opportunity to get to know people, exchange ideas, find out new things. Ninety-five percent of people are basically nice and would be more communicative if the activation energy to start the process was there. So instead of moaning about what a fuckedup world we live in, as artists have been doing for the past 200 years, I want to actually do something about it. Although it's a total drop in the ocean, *Talkaoke* and the other projects I'm involved in try to address the problem by changing it, not by 'critiquing it' – art student terminology.

This has a political dimension too. Contemporary mass culture is in love with voting and democracy – as long as they can set the agenda. If you're voting for which page three girl's got the nicest tits (*The Sun*, December 8, 2004), who wins *Pop Idol* or what colour you want your government to be, that's fine. But you can't set the agenda. This reinforces the power relationship. TV especially subjugates us. TV invades our psyche, our dreams, we're not in control. When I ring up a radio-phone show my heart is pounding, I start to sweat, I don't like that. It should belong to us. I want people to feel they can participate on their own terms.

SM: What have been the high and low points of doing Talkaoke, and what themes or discussions have particularly stood out?

ME: *Talkaoke* is an invitation for people to come together and socialise, so it kind of depends on who's there when it's set up. These days if it's not a quality show I blame everybody who's there – not just me. Sometimes people want to attack me or criticise me or give me a hard time. There was a show I did at the opening of the Pandaemonium festival, also at the Vibe Bar in Brick Lane in 1998 or 1999. It was a whole load of drunken video artists having a go at me. The whole mood of the

Talkaoke,
1997–present
Photograph courtesy
of the artist

event was pernicious. Because other people were doing it, people decided the point of the show was to attack me, make it difficult for the show to flow, somehow teach me a lesson for having such a big ego. Paradoxically it tends to be the most self-obsessed people who accuse me of being egoistic. I felt shit at the end of that show and was very surprised to learn that people really enjoyed it. After the Edinburgh festival I was psychologically so exhausted that it took months to recover.

SM: I feel great every time Talkaoke comes together and people who are honest about their half-formed ideas try to make a full idea together. Can you talk about your 'practice' and how you see yourself as an artist, but also as a kind of entrepreneur, as Talkaoke is a business too?

MW: One of my favourite things to talk about is how you are supposed to make money as an artist. When I was at college the tutors used their own 'practice' as inspiration. This seemed a little hypocritical to me, because they made their money mainly by teaching us. We couldn't do what they did because they already had the academic jobs. There should be more focus on how to create a market for yourself. It seems you have a choice of either sucking up to the big institutions or very rich individuals. These people have 95% of the influence over what is considered contemporary art. To a large extent they determine the agenda. Artists are like sheep in a field. The curators are the shepherds deciding which one to take to the county show and which one to have for breakfast. The rest of the artists just stand

and munch grass. So the big guys set the agenda. This is a lot better than mass culture, where corporate interests set the agenda. Of recent times I have preferred state artists – those who have made a reputation whilst being in academic positions or in receipt of government grants.

In this situation as one of the sheep I decided I had to develop my own income so as not to be dependent on either the government, institutions, wealthy individuals or large corporations. I have never been so depressed as when I was a gallery artist putting on 'groundbreaking' shows every two months in cold empty spaces, looking up expectantly at the door every time someone walked in (every two hours) in the vain hope it was Saatchi. I realised that by selling *Talkaoke* as a form of entertainment that people pay for on a nightly basis I could be free of the above constraints. By their nature institutions have to have a framework in which they relate to an artist, which is fixed and can only be changed by a committee. I find this impossible to deal with. Funding bodies ask all the wrong questions. I don't blame them. It's an institutional procedure. By honing *Talkaoke* as a product, it is a true endorsement of my work. If people are willing to pay for it directly, it is what it gives them.

It's selling direct to the public, except not really, because it tends to be councils, festival organisers etc. that hire *Talkaoke*. This way of selling *Talkaoke* has constrained my development of other projects however because it requires a lot of input and professionalism. It's difficult to introduce new ideas into this environment because it requires my own investment of the profits of *Talkaoke* into research and development and it takes up a lot of time running a business. I have a number of new projects on the go, germinating slowly so it does work in the long term.

Sarah McCrory

Mark Wayman

Mark Wayman's performances are conceived as guided tours around unspectacular places such as private houses, backyards and the unseen spaces in art galleries and sites of historical interest. Wayman concentrates on architectural details, exploring his chosen sites through their less significant features and the marks left by time. The artist's meticulous monologues, a kind of verbal scanning, reveal the place's particular appearance and potential, altering our perception of the space around us.

Wayman looks at architectural spaces as structures, imbued with hidden, often unacknowledged, histories. He chooses a site for his performance and then memorises its details, in order to give a deadpan descriptive tour of the place. These descriptions, which might be seen as archaeological studies of the present, do not directly refer to what the audience is looking at. Wayman uses different strategies to detach his words from the scene he is pointing to. He seems to forget a detail here, ignore another there and to be somewhat vague. This behaviour forces the audience to pay attention and carefully notice their surroundings. Over the course of Wayman's guided tour, the audience slowly becomes aware of the gap between what they are looking at and what they are hearing about. This moment of realisation is at the heart of Wayman's performances.

Memorator, 2000
Part of Theatre of
Memory, Theatre
of Myth Plunge Club
24-hour event
Photograph courtesy
of the artist

Memory Aids for
Invertor, 2000
Courtesy of the artist

In *Invertor* (2000), performed at Toynbee Studios, London, Wayman took the audience on a tour down the building's staircase, highlighting features such as the number of steps and the colour of the walls. The objects he described, however, did not match the objects he was indicating, which were not referred to at all. For only a brief moment, at the centre of the performance, did Wayman's account match the actual features of the building. At this point the audience began to notice the structural features that Wayman had mentioned earlier and it became clear that he had inverted his description of the staircase, so that it ran in the opposite direction to the tour.

For *Shifter* (2000) Wayman memorised the appearance of the South London Gallery's walled backyard. Wearing a blindfold, he described the structural details of the area in intimate detail, but his description became increasingly disconnected from the objects to which he pointed, as he lost his orientation in the space. What he described was there, but there was a gap between the words and the objects, making the viewer acutely aware of the physical details of his surroundings.

The incongruity between what Wayman describes and his own location in space, the omissions and inversions he employs, and his memory's own flaws, are tactics he uses to sharpen our sense of the world. When our visual perception of reality and Wayman's description of it get out of sync, an *unheimlich* sense of an infinite number of possible realities seeps in.

Alejandra Aguado

Biographies

Sachiko Abe

Born 1975 in Nara
Lives and works in Fukuoka

Selected Solo Exhibitions

2005 Gallery SOAP, Fukuoka
Navigate, Performance Festival, Baltic
Centre for Contemporary Art,
Newcastle
2004 Laura Bartlett Gallery, London
Bluecoat Arts Centre, Liverpool (in
conjunction with Liverpool Biennial)
2001 *To Inside…*, Former Hyakusanjyu
Bank Gallery, Kitakyushu

Selected Group Exhibitions

2004 *Cut Papers*, PS1 Contemporary Art
Center program studio, New York
Touchable Painting, Ueno-no Mori Art
Mueum, Tokyo
2002 *Error – Error*, Fukuoka Art
Museum, Fukuoka
Library Project, Sendai Mediatheque,
Sendai
Danger Map, Gallery SOAP, Kitakyushu
and Japan Expo., Tokyo

Johanna Billing

Born 1973 in Jönköping
Lives and works in Stockholm

Selected Solo Exhibitions

2004 *You Don't Love Me Yet*, Vedanta
Gallery, Chicago
2003 *Studio Works*, Milch at
Gainsborough Studios, London
You Don't Love Me Yet, Index,
Stockholm
2001 *Where She Is At*, Moderna Museet
Projekt/Oslo Kunsthall, Oslo
2000 *Project for a Revolution*, Galleri
Flach, Stockholm

Selected Group Exhibitions

2004 *Delayed on Time*, Museum of
Contemporary Art, Zagreb
The Yugoslav Biennial of Young Artists,
Vrsac
The Edstrandska Foundation Prize, Malmö
Konsthall, Malmö
Delays and Revolutions, Venice Biennale,
Italian Pavilion, Venice
2002 *Paus*, Gwangju Biennale, Gwangju

Bibliography

2005 *Johanna Billing*, Jan Verwoert,
Moscow Biennale Catalogue
2004 *Between indecision and optimism*,
from *A future that might have worked*,
Nada Beros for *Delayed on time*
Catalogue, Museum of Contemporary
Art, Zagreb

Pavel Braìla

Born 1971 in Chisinau
Lives and works in Chisinau

Selected Solo Exhibitions

2005 MIT List Visual Arts Center,
Cambridge, Massachusetts
2004 *33 Revolutions per Minute*,
Galerie Yvon Lambert, Paris
2003 *Performance White or Pale
Unfinished Thoughts*, Kunstbuero,
Vienna
2001 *Gedankenaufnahme*, Pavel Braìla,
Kunstbüro, Vienna

Selected Group Exhibitions

2004 *The Balkans – A Crossroad to the
Future*, Arte Fiera, Bologna
Cine y Casi Cine, Museo Nacional
Centro de Arte Reina Sofia, Madrid
2003 *New Video, New Europe*, The
Renaissance Society, Chicago, Illinois
2002 *Documenta 11*, Kassel
1999 *After The Wall: Art and Culture in
Post-Communist Europe*, Moderna
Museet, Stockholm

Bibliography

2005 'Pavel Braìla', exhibtion catalogue,
MIT List Visual Arts Center,
ed. Jane Farver, David Freilach,
Cambridge, Mass.

Lali Chetwynd
Born 1973 in London
Lives and works in London

Selected Solo Shows
2005 *Debt*, a Medieval Play, Beck's
  Futures, ICA , London
2004 *Born Free – The Death of a*
  Conservationist, Gasworks Gallery,
  London
2003 *An Evening With Jabba the Hutt*,
  International 3, Manchester

Selected Group Shows
2004 *Erotics and Bestiality*,
  New Contemporaries, Liverpool
  Biennial
2003 *Aelita Queen of Mars – Kabinett*
  der Abstrakten, Bloomberg SPACE,
  London
The Hulk, Vilma Gold Presents,
  Vilma Gold, London
Richard Dadd and the Dance of Death,
  The Golden Resistance, Tate & Egg Live,
  Tate Britain, London
2002 *Thriller, Fertility Dance – Atatque*
  De Nervios, Hoxton Hall, London

Bibliography
2005 'Beck's Futures', ICA, London
2004 'Review of International 3
  Performance', by Neil Mulholland,
  Flash Art, vol XXXVII, no 234, Jan/Feb

Kim Coleman
Born 1976 in Edinburgh
Lives and works in Edinburgh

Selected Solo Exhibitions
and performances
2005 *Speech is Silver*, National Galleries
  of Scotland
2004 *Timeless*, Collective Gallery,
  Edinburgh
Amazing Grace, Glasgow

Selected Group Exhibitions
and Performances
2004 *Editions*, Lowry Gallery,
  Manchester
Not Yet Night, The Ship, London
Amaryllis sillyramA, GSS, Glasgow
2003 *Late at Tate*, Tate Britain, London
Platform, Waygood, Newcastle
Women Men Children, Transmission
  Gallery, Glasgow
2002 *The Chateau*, Switchspace, Glasgow

Robin Deacon
Born 1973 in Eastbourne
Lives and works in Bedford and London

Selected Performances
2004 *Colin Powell*, About Time, Project
  Arts Centre, Dublin
True Stories, Fierce Earth Festival,
  Repertory Theatre, Birmingham
2003 *Unit/Speech*, Art & Food, Victoria
  and Albert Museum, London
National Review of Live Art, The Arches,
  Glasgow
Hard Water and Other Objects, PS7
  (The Seventh Performance Studies
  Conference), University of Mainz
Acme, Exit, The Cable Factory, Helsinki
I am a Man, Gooseflesh, Rakvere
The Costello Show, Push Festival,
  Young Vic Theatre, London.
1996 *Bobby Valentine: The Man*,
  European Media Art Festival,
  Osnabruck
1995 *The Attack of the Killer Cheeses*,
  Exhibitionists, ICA, London

Bilbliography
2004 'The Performance Pack', J. Sofaer,
  Tate Publishing
'Performing Difference', R. Okon,
  Artsadmin

www.robindeacon.com

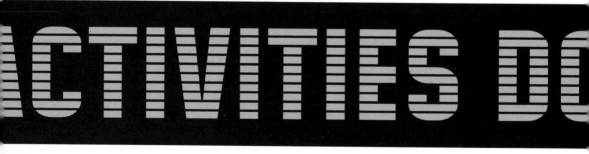

Richard Dedomenici
Born 1978 in Hexham
Lives and works in London

Selected performances

2005 *Stay*, site-specific work at Great
Eastern Hotel, London
Embracing Failure, 18–19 January,
lecture at BAC London
2004 *Boris*, street performance for the
Liverpool Biennial
Anti, Performance Festival, Kuopio
Duckie, Performance Royal Vauxhall
Tavern, London
Express Excess, support act for John
Hegley at the Enterprise, Chalk Farm
Version04, Annual Art festival, Chicago
2003 *Sexed-Up*, East England Arts'artist-in-
residence Edinburgh Fringe
Writing DNA, Wellcome Trust/TwoTen
Gallery, London
2002 National Review of Live Art,
Glasgow

Bibliography

2005 'Oops,he did it again', Rhodri
Marsden, *The Guardian*, 17 January

Harrell Fletcher
Born 1967 in Santa Maria, California
Lives and works in Portland, Oregon

Selected Solo Exhibitions

2005 Laura Bartlett Gallery, London
2004 *Hi*, Christine Burgin Gallery,
New York
Maintaining the Jazz, Jack Hanley Gallery,
San Francisco
2003 *Reread Summerhill*, Signal Art
Center, Malmö
2001 *Everyday Sunshine*, Portland
Institute for Contemporary Art, Oregon

Selected Group Exhibitions

2004 Whitney Biennial, Whitney
Museum, New York
2003 *Baja to Vancouver*, The Seattle Art
Museum, Seattle
Street Selections, The Drawing Center,
New York
2002 *Playground*, Institute of
Contemporary Art at MECA, Portland,
Maine
*Of the Moment: Contemporary Art from
the Collection,* SFMOMA,
San Francisco

Bibliography

2004 'Harrell Fletcher: New Langton
Arts/Jack Hanley Gallery', Glen
Helfand, *Artforum*, May
'Harrell Fletcher at the Christine Burgin
Gallery', Holland Cotter, *The New York
Times*, 28 May

David Hatcher
Born 1973 in Auckland
Lives and works in Berlin and Los Angeles

Selected Solo Exhibitions

2004 *Oedipal Manoeuvres in the Dark*,
müllerdechiara, Berlin
Philosophical Investigations (with et al.),
Starkwhite, Auckland
2003 *Standard Deviations*, Lippische
Gesellschaft für Kunst, Detmold
2002 *Black Fluffy Clouds*, ABEL Raum
für Neue Kunst, Berlin

Selected Group Exhibitions

2005 *Empire Style*, 2102, Los Angeles
Echo/Anti-Echo, Galerie Barbara
Thumm, Berlin
2004 *A Complete Guide to Rewriting
Your History*, Sparwasser HQ, Berlin
Black Friday. Exercises in Hermetics,
Galerie Kamm, Berlin
2003 *The Sky's the Limit*, Kunstverein
Langenhagen, Langenhagen
*Dasein – Positionen zeitgenössischer Kunst
aus der Sammlung Reinking*, Ernst-
Barlach-Museum, Ratzeburg and Wedel

Bibliography

2005 *David Hatcher – I DON'T MUST*
(ed. Astrid Mania), Rooseum Center for
Contemporary Art, Malmö, and
Revolver Archiv für aktuelle Kunst,
Frankfurt
David Hatcher and John Baldessari,
'It came from between red and yellow',
in: *Neue Review, Art in Berlin*, Issue 9

www.harrellfletcher.com
www.learningtoloveyoumore.com

Jenny Hogarth

Born 1979 in Glasgow
Lives and works in Glasgow

Selected Solo Exhibitions

2004 *Pentland Rising*, Midlothian Ski
Centre, Hillend (commissioned by the
Collective Gallery, Edinburgh)
2002 *Rest Sweet Nymphs*, Where the
Monkey Sleeps, Glasgow
2001 *Does This Sound Like Something
You've Heard Before?,* Collective
Gallery, Edinburgh

Selected Group Exhibitions

2005 *Timeless*, the Glasgow Project
Rooms, Glasgow (with Babak Ghazi and
Kim Coleman)
Conquests and Techniques: A Synthesis,
The Ship, London
2004 *The Embassy Collection II*,
Thermo 04, The Lowry, Manchester
Ganghut, weekend event by Kevin Reid,
Spike Island, Bristol
Amaryllis sillyramA and Demonstration,
Glasgow Sculpture Studios, Glasgow
2003 *Late at the Tate*, Tate Britain, London
Men Women Children, Tramsmission
Gallery, Glasgow

Emily Jacir

Born 1970
Lives and works in Ramallah and New York

Selected Solo Exhibitions

2005 *Accumulations*, Alexander and
Bonin, New York
Anthony Reynolds Gallery, London
2004 *Emily Jacir: Where We Come From*,
Moderna Museet, Stockholm and
The Khalil Sakakini Cultural Centre,
Ramallah
2003 *Belongings*, OK Center for
Contemporary Art, Linz

Selected Group Exhibitions

2005 Padiglione Italia, 50th Venice
Biennale, Venice
2004 Whitney Biennial, Whitney Museum
of American Art, New York
Wherever I Am, Modern Art, Oxford
This Much is Certain, Royal College of Art,
London
2003 Istanbul Biennale, Istanbul

Bibliography

2004 'VV AA, Emily Jacir: Belongings.
Arbeiten/Works 1998–2003', Folio
Verlag Wien
2003 'Desire in Diaspora: Emily Jacir',
T.J. Demos, *Art Journal*, Winter,
pp 68–78

Jesper Just

Born 1974 in Copenhagen
Lives and works in Copenhagen

Selected Solo Exhibitions

2004 YYZ Gallery, Toronto
Bliss and Heaven, Maze Gallery, Turin
Perry Rubenstein Gallery, New York
A Fine Romance, Galleri Christina Wilson,
Copenhagen
2003 *The Man who Strayed*, Den anden
opera & Artnode, Copenhagen

Selected Group Exhibitions

2004 *MALM I*, Malmö Konsthall
Fabulation, VOX, Montreal
3rd Momentum, Nordic Festival of
Contemporary Art, Moss
2003 *Something about Love*, Casino
Luxembourg, Luxembourg
BIG Social Game, GAM Gallery of Modern
and Contemporary Art, Turin

Bibliography

2005 'Reflections in a Glass Curtain',
Andrea Bellini, *Flash Art*, January –
February, Vol XXXVIII
2004 'Jesper Just', Max Andrews, *Frieze*,
June, July, August, vol 84, p 139

Leopold Kessler

Born 1976 in Munich
Lives and works in Vienna

Selected Solo Exhibitions

2003 *Synchronization*, Offspace, Vienna
Privatisert, Galerie Corentin Hamel,
Paris

Selected Group Exhibitions

2004 Manifesta 05, San Sebastian
Personne n'est innocent..., Confort
Modern, Poitier
Niemandsland, Künstlerhaus, Vienna
2003 *VV2*, 50th Venice Biennale, Venice
Critique is not enough, Shedhalle, Zürich
Haunted by Detail, Stichting de Appel,
Amsterdam

Deimantas Narkevičius

Born 1964 in Utena
Lives and works in Vilnius

Selected Solo Exhibitions

2004 *An Exhibition of Two Sculptures*,
Contemporary Art Centre, Vilnius
The Role of a Lifetime, Gallery Foksal,
Warsaw
2003 *Either True or Fictitious*, Frac des
Pays de la Loire, Nantes
2002 *Deimantas Narkevicius project*,
Münchner Kunstverein, Munich and
GB Agency, Paris
2001 The Lithuanian Pavillion, 49th
Venice Biennale, Venice

Selected Group Exhibitions

2004 *Europa, Film and Video from the
Centre of Europe*, Tate Modern, London
Time and Again, Stedelijk Museum,
Amsterdam
*Two Films: Anna Klamroth and Deimantas
Narkevicius*, Dundee Contemporary
Art, Dundee
2003 *Displacements*, Musée d'Art
Moderne de le Ville de Paris, Paris
The Viewer's Dictatorship, 50th Venice
Biennale, Venice

Bibliography

2003 Hans-Ulrich Obrist, Interview with
Diemantas Narkevicius, *Flash Art*,
October
'Home truths. How do you portray
a historical crisis', Jan Verwoert on
Deimantas Narkevicius, *Frieze*,
issue 72, January – February

Roman Ondák

Born 1966 in Zilina
Lives and works in Bratislava

Selected Solo Exhibitions

2004 *Spirit and Opportunity*, Kölnischer
Kunstververein, Cologne
2003 *Another Day*, Dum umeni, Brno
2002 *Guided Tour*, Moderna Galerija,
Zagreb
2000 *MK Gallery*, Rotterdam

Selected Group Exhibitions

2005 *Universal Experience: Art, Life and
the Tourist's Eye*, Museum of
Contemporary Art, Chicago
2004 *Time and Again*, Stedelijk Museum,
Amsterdam
Frieze Art Fair Projects, Frieze Art Fair,
London
2003 *Beautiful Banners*, Prague Biennial,
Prague
Utopia Station, 50th Venice Biennale,
Venice

Bibliography

2005 'First Take', Jessica Morgan,
Artforum International, January
2003 'Cream 3', Igor Zabel, Phaidon Press

Michael Rakowitz

Born 1973 in New York
Lives and works in New York

Selected Solo Exhibitions

1998–2005 *paraSITE*, Ongoing project in various urban sites in Boston, New York

2004 *Greetings from Stowe, Vermont*, Kunstraum Innsbruck/Stadtturmgalerie

2003 *Romanticised All Out of Proportion*, Special Project, Queens Museum of Art, New York

2002 *Breach Lower East Side*, Tenement Museum, New York

2001 *Climate Control*, Special Project, P.S.1 Contemporary Art Center, New York

Selected Group Exhibitions

2005 *SAFE: Design Takes on Risk*, MoMA, New York

2004 *Parasites: When Spaces Come into Play*, Museum of Modern Art Foundation Ludwig, Vienna

The Interventionists, MassMOCA, North Adams

2003 *BQE*, White Box, New York

Get Rid of Yourself, ACC Gallery, Weimar and Leipzig

Bibliography

2003 'Michael Rakowitz: Circumventions', published by onestar press/Dena Foundation, Paris

Reader

Eilidh MacAskill born 1980 in Glasgow
Lives and works in Glasgow
Robert Walton born 1980 in Burnley
Lives and works in Glasgow
Lalage Harries born 1977 in London
Lives and works Glasgow
James Leadbitter born 1980 in Burnley
Lives and works in London
Group formed at Dartington College of Arts, 2001

Selected Performances

2005 *Strangers and Intimacy*, West Space Gallery, Melbourne

2004 *Hugger-Mugger*, Chandler Studio, Royal Scottish Academy of Music and Drama, Glasgow

Songs from the Burning Bed: Song minus One – Cock of the Walk, CCA, Glasgow

2003 *Warm Welcome Cold Climate*, CCA, Glasgow

Base Camp II, Edinburgh Sculpture Workshop, Edinburgh

Dumb Bunny, Tramway, Glasgow (A Tramway Dark Lights Commission)

A Meeting to Decide the Nature of a New Planet and its Contents, Mono Café, Glasgow

2002 *Special Relationship*, SYHA Youth Hostel (for EmergeD)

Your Hand on my Skin and the Earth's Still Turning, Brunel University, Dartington College of Art and The Arches, Glasgow

Mr. Pig says 'Out with the Old', Tramway, Glasgow

Giorgio Sadotti

Born 20th century in Stockport
Lives and works in London

Selected Solo Exhibitions

2004 *I Believe in Everything*, Kunst Redux, London

2003 *Untitled*, Platform, London

Perpetual Euphoria, with Paul Noble, Elektra House, London

1999 *Went to America Didn't Say a Word*, Space, London

Selected Group Exhibitions

2005 *A to Z and Back Again*, Galerie Chez Valentin, Paris

Romantic Detachment, Chapter Arts, Cardiff and PS1, MoMA, New York

2004 *Russian Doll*, MOT, London

2001 *Century City*, Tate Modern, London

Protest and Survive, Whitechapel Gallery, London.

Bibliography

2002 'City Racing; The Life and Times Of An Artist-Run Gallery', Black Dog Publishing Limited, pp 5–17

1996–7 'Documents sur L'art', no 10, Winter, pp 14–22

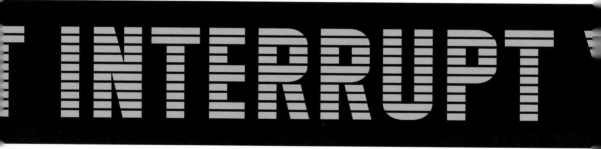

Bibliography

2005 'The Act of Reading (and the Fire Next Time)', Stephen J. Bottoms, Westspace Gallery, Melbourne

www.readreader.org

Yara El-Sherbini
Born 1978 in Derbyshire
Lives and works in London

Selected Performances

2003 *Hit me,* 9th Cairo International
Biennale, Cairo
Rooted and re-routed, as part of
Hom(e)age, Soho Theatre, London
Narratives Dublin Fringe Festival, Dublin
Ex-Centris, Tate Modern, London
Traces, National Review of Live Art,
Glasgow
Narratives of the other Inbetween Time
Festival, Arnolfini, Bristol
2002 *Vacant Lot,* Spike Island, Bristol

Selected Exhibitions

2003 *Artist Survival Kit,* Hotel Bellville,
London
Aiding and Abetting, Birkbeck College,
London
Mute-Dialogue project. Watershed, Bristol

Bibliography

2005 'Yara El-Sherbini 'Sheikh n Vac',
Bookworks, London

Christian Sievers
Born 1974 in Braunschweig
Lives and works in London

Selected Solo Exhibitions

2003 *Cleaner,* Liverpool Street Station,
London
2002–5 *The Christian Sievers News of
the World Monthly Update,* London,
Edinburgh, Berlin
2002 *Henna Tattoos for Everyone,*
Nebenraum and Alexanderplatz, Berlin
2000 *In Case I Get Hurt,* HBK
Braunschweig

Selected Group Exhibitions

2005 *Show One,* Werst, London
2004 *The Retrospective. Abramovic Class
1997–2004,* HBK Braunschweig
2003 *Cold Stew,* VTO Gallery, London
2002 *Militant,* Postfuhramt, Berlin
2001 *Kunststudenten stellen aus,*
Kunst- und Ausstellungshalle der
Bundesrepublik Deutschland, Bonn

Bibliography

2003 'On Sleeping in Public & Being
Cautious', London
'Student Body', ed. Marina Abramovic,
Santiago de Compostela

www.christiansievers.info

Song Dong
Born 1966 in Beijing
Lives and works in Beijing

Selected Solo Exhibitions

2004 *Water Works,* Chinese Arts Centre,
Manchester
2002 *Chopsticks: Song Dong and Yin
Xiuzhen,* Chambers Fine Art, New York
Eyeball, Beijing International Switching
System Corporation Ltd., BISC,
Beijing
2000 *Song Dong in London,* Tablet
Gallery, London
1994 *Another Lesson: Do You Want to
Play with Me?,* installation show
and performance, Central Academy
of Fine Arts Gallery, Beijing

Selected Group Exhibitions

2004 26th São Paolo Bienal, São Paolo
2003 8th Istanbul Biennial, Istanbul
2002 4th Gwangju Biennale, Gwangju
4th Asia-Pacific Triennial of Contemporary
Art (APT), Queensland Art
Gallery, Queensland
4th Guangzhou Triennial, Guangdong
Museum of Art, Guangzhou

Bibliography

2002 'Chopsticks Yin Xiuzhen, Song
Dong', Editors: Christophe W. Mao,
Song Dong, Yin Xiuzhen, Chambers
Fine Art, New York
2000 'Fuck Off', editors: Hua Tianxue,
Ai Weiwei, Feng Boyi, Eastlink Gallery,
Shanghai

Kate Stannard
Born 1981 in Penrith
Lives and works in Glasgow

Selected Performances
2004 *Missing Things 2*, Commissioned by
the Merchant City Festival, Glasgow
Flesh and Blood, Guest director with
Primus Theatre Company, Cumbria
Dirty Girls Need...Soap, An ongoing series
of works, in collaboration with artist
Sarah Potter, CCA Lab Night, Arches
Club Night and Tramway Freespace,
Glasgow
Missing Things, The National Review of
Live Art 2004, Glasgow
2003 *Ties That Bind*, Royal Scottish
Academy of Music and Drama, Glasgow
Lifedrawing: 2, Commissioned by Belluad
Bollwerk International Festival and
FRI ART, Fribourg
This Far No Further, Tramway, Glasgow
(as part of Into the New 2003)
Lifedrawing, National Review of Live Art
2003, Glasgow
2002 *Lifedrawing*, Tramway, Glasgow
(as part of Into the New 2002)

www.katestannard.co.uk

Talkaoke (Michael Weinkove)
Born 1974 in Reading
Lives and works in London

Selection group exhibitions
2004 *Bitflows*, new media conference
and exhibition, Vienna
Splice Live, Liverpool Biennial
2003 *Art for Networks*, Chapter Gallery,
Cardiff
2001 *Century City*, Tate Modern, London
1998 *Bank TV*, London
1997 *The Bank*, London
1997–04 *Aconvention*, performed at
Edinburgh Festival, Sonar Festival,
London Sci-fi, Future Wales, Creative
Links

Selected Collaborators
2002 Saul Albert of London Wireless
Network, developed The People Speak
Network
1998–01 James Stevens of Backspace,
developed mobile web-casting
technologies for Talkaoke

Bibliography
2000 *Evening Standard Magazine*, 2 June

www.talkaoke.com

Mark Wayman
Born 1964 in Sutton Coldfield
Lives and works in London

Selected Performances
2002 *MicrOrcram*, Home, Camberwell,
London
Reflector, Bolt Cellar Lane Hedge, near
Epping, Essex
2000 *Memorator*, in *Theatre of Memory*,
Theatre of Myth, Plunge Club, London
Invertor, Toynbee Hall, London
Shifter, South London Gallery, London
1999 *Slips*, Project Space, London
The Pillar and Post of Dickory Dockney, in
My Old Man, The Rosemary Branch
Theatre, London
1998 *Bi nt'ring a kynd ov 'stayte'*, *Mystr
Wayman wil goh in thu fabrik ov thu
rume ann attempit ta sukky owt frome itt
wotsoe'er lyz ther diplee berid*, ICA,
London
1997 *In and Out of the Light*, The Rack
Gallery, London
Double Booking, (with Lawrence Harvey),
in *Connected Showcase*, The Northern
Gallery for Contemporary Arts,
Sunderland

Bibliography
'Salon 27', Mark Wayman, 'micrOrcam'
www.lgihome.co.uk/salon27_kitchen.htm

Works in the Exhibition

Sachiko Abe

Cut Papers, 2005
Live installation, cotton, gauze, paper,
scissors, microphone and speakers
Dimensions variable
Courtesy of Laura Bartlett Gallery,
London

Johanna Billing

Where she is at, 2001
Video (DV PAL)
7 min 35 sec on a loop
Courtesy of the artist

Pavel Braïla

Recalling Events, 2000
DV transferred onto DVD, 4 min
Courtesy of Galerie Yvon Lambert, Paris
and the artist

Lali Chetwynd

*Pasta Necklace Workshop (Advance
Classes in Bronze Age Jewellery)*, 2005
Performance

Kim Coleman and Jenny Hogarth

Not Yet Titled, 2005
Performance
Commissioned for
Do Not Interrupt Your Activities

Robin Deacon

Colin Powell, 2004–2005
Performance, 1 hr

Richard Dedomenici

Embracing Failure, 2004
Lecture Performance, 1 hr
Commissioned by New Work Network
Continuing Your Journey, 2005
Performance, 1 day durational event
Commissioned for
Do Not Interrupt Your Activities

Harrell Fletcher

Come Together (London) 9 April, 2005
Afternoon Lecture Programme. 14 ten-
minute lectures by 14 different people.
Orange Girl Picture, 2005
Lambda print and latex paint, white
wooden frame, 76.2 × 101.5 cm
Courtesy of Laura Bartlett Gallery
Newspapers, 1998–2005
Dimensions variable
Courtesy of the artist
Hello There Friend, 2004
Film on DVD, 18 min
Courtesy of the artist

David Hatcher

Holding Pattern, 1998
11 Engraved acrylic plaques
Dimensions variable each *c.*7 × 18 cm
Collection of Charlotte Armstrong and
Anthony Drumm, Berlin

Emily Jacir

Sexy Semite, 2000–2002
Documentation of an intervention
Shelf, newspapers, framed cuttings
Overall dimensions 100 × 185 cm
Edition of 3
Courtesy Anthony Reynolds Gallery,
London

Jesper Just

The Lonely Villa, 2004
16mm film transferred to video,
5 min 30 sec
Edition of 10 + 2 AP
Courtesy of Perry Rubenstein Gallery,
New York

Leopold Kessler

Privatized, 2001–2003
Video of intervention
Repaired, 2002
Video of intervention
Intercom, 2003
Video of intervention
Akademiekable, 2004
Video of intervention
Secured, 2005
Video of intervention
Commissioned for
Do Not Interrupt Your Activities
All works courtesy of the artist and
Corentin Hamel Gallery, Paris

Deimantas Narkevičius
Once in the XX Century, 2004
　Betacam SP video printed on DVD,
　8 min
　Courtesy gb agency, Jan Mot
　and the artist

Roman Ondák
Announcement, 2002
　Sound installation, radio set, radio
　broadcast on CD
　Repeated every 4 min 30 sec
　on a loop
　Courtesy of gb agency, Paris and
　Gallery Martin Janda, Vienna

Michael Rakowitz
paraSITE, 1998–ongoing
　Dimensions variable
　Courtesy of the artist and
　Lombard-Freid Gallery, New York

Reader
'Can't you hear me? It's dark in here.
Where have you gone anyway?':
Weathering the storms of human relations:
A symposium, 2005
　Durational performance event
　Commissioned for
　Do Not Interrupt Your Activities

Giorgio Sadotti
Went To America Didn't Say a Word, 1999
　Sound installation, speakers, 19 CDs,
　audio equipment, 23 hr 26 min
　Courtesy of the artist
Violin Siren, 2004
　Sound sculpture duration variable
　Courtesy of the artist

Yara El-Sherbini
A Demonstration, 2005
　Performance
　Commissioned for
　Do Not Interrupt Your Activities

Christian Sievers
On Look but Don't Touch, 2005
　Lecture 15 min
　Commissioned for
　Do Not Interrupt Your Activities

Song Dong
Writing Diary with Water, 1995–present
　Four photographs 59 × 39 cm
　Courtesy of the artist
You Can Write Anything with Water
on Stone, 2004
　Installation dimensions variable
　Courtesy of the artist

Kate Stannard
Missing Things 1 & 2, 2004–2005
　Durational performance and installation
Missing Things 1, A 'one year on'
　commission for The National Review
　of Live Art, 2004, performed at
　The Arches, Glasgow, with support
　from CCA, February 2004
Missing Things 2, Performed as part of the
　Merchant City Festival, Glasgow, in
　connection with The National Review
　of Live Art, produced by New Moves
　International, September 2004

Talkaoke (Michael Weinkove)
Talkaoke, 1997–present
　Live event
　Courtesy of the artist

Mark Wayman
Memorial, 2005
　Performance, 20mins.
　Commissioned for
　Do Not Interrupt Your Activities

Acknowledgements

With special thanks to:

all the artists and their galleries
the first year CCA students
Astrid Mania

and course staff:
David Batchelor
Claire Bishop
Michaela Crimmin
Alex Farquharson
Jean Fisher
Teresa Gleadowe
Fiona Key
Loveday Shewell
Dominic Willsdon

We would also like to thank:

Michael Alexander
Claudia Amthor-Croft
Alessio Antoniolli
Salvatore Aranciog
Charlotte Armstrong
Laura Bartlett
Danny Bierset
Conrad Bodman
Peter Bonnel
Fiona Boundy
Elaine Bowen
John Bracken
Sue Bradburn
Daniel Brine
Christine Burgin
Laura Carter
Maria Charalambous
Sylvia Chivaratanond
Martin Clark
Henry Coleman
Padraig Coogan
Ann Coxon
Ben Craze
Paul Cross
Peter Cross
Paul Cruse
Anthony Drumm
Áine Duffy
Dominic Feuchs
Stuart Franey
Chris Franklin
Prof. Sir Christopher Frayling

Lea Fried
Richard Grayson
Chris Gordon
Manick Govinda
Corentin Hamel
Jack Hanley
Tasmin Head
Matthew Higgs
Alistair Hudson
William Hunt
John Johnson
Lois Keidan
Vasif Kortun
Sally Lai
Ash Lange
Simon Levine
Ray Martin
Eddie Marsh
John McCormack
Cuauhtémoc Medina
Frances Morris
Danielle Mourning
Mark Nash
Chris Nelms
Alistair Noonan
Rupert Norfolk
Roman Ondák
Su-Lin Ong
Garry Philpott
Greg Philpott
Greg Piggot
Silke Pillinger

Vanessa Rolf
Nigel Rolfe
Polly Staple
Lisa Stewart
Adam Sutherland
Sally Tallant
Junko Takekawa
Simon Taylor
Nicky Verber
Jan Verwoert
Alex Watt
Mark Wayman
Ian White
Peter B. Willberg
Catherine Wood
David Wright

The title of this exhibition derives, in amended and abbreviated form, from *Announcement* (2002), a work by Roman Ondák.

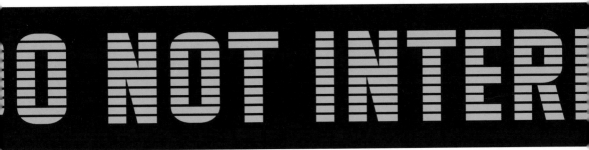

Do Not Interrupt Your Activities
was curated by graduating
students on the MA Curating Contemporary
Art at the Royal College of Art:

Alejandra Aguado
Gair Boase
Anna Colin
Lillian Davies
Carmen Juliá
Rose Lejeune
James Lindon
Ali MacGilp
Rebecca May Marston
Sarah McCrory
Aaron Moulton
Cassandra Needham
Giselle Richardson

Catalogue written, compiled
and edited by the curators.

Editorial supervision:
Claire Bishop
Teresa Gleadowe
Fiona Key
Astrid Mania

Designed by Peter B. Willberg
assisted by Maria Charalambous
at Clarendon Road Studio
Printed by Specialblue
Printed on Essential Velvet,
supplied by Premier Paper

Published by the
Royal College of Art, London, 2005
Texts © 2005 Royal College of Art
and the authors

ISBN 1-905000-11-1

RUPT ACTIVIT